TRUE STORIE:
IN SIX GENERATIC

M000167353

HANNAH'S
Girls
Ruthie
(Born 1931)

Ruth Vitrano Merkel

REVIEW AND HERALD® PUBLISHING ASSOCIATION
HAGERSTOWN, MD 21740

The Review and Herald® Publishing Association publishes biblically based materials for spiritual, physical, and mental growth and Christian discipleship.

The author assumes full responsibility for the accuracy of all facts and quotations as cited in this book.

Texts credited to NIV are from the *Holy Bible, New International Version.* Copyright © 1973, 1978, 1984, International Bible Society. Used by permission of Zondervan Bible Publishers.

This book was
Edited by Penny Estes Wheeler
Cover design by Trent Truman
Cover illustration by Matthew Archambault
Electronic makeup Shirley M. Bolivar
Typeset: Goudy 13/16

PRINTED IN U.S.A.

11 10 09 08 07   5 4 3 2 1

R&H Cataloging Service
Merkel, Ruth Vitrano
    Ruthie

    1. Seventh-day Adventists—Biography.   2. Seventh-day Adventists—History.   I. Title   II. Series: Hannah's Girls

286.73209

ISBN: 978-0-8280-1954-5

Dedication

To my daughters,
Elaine and Marcia
&
To my grandchildren,
Erin, Benjamin, and Bradley

Other books in the *Hannah's Girls* series, by Ruth Vitrano Merkel:

Hannah's Girls: Ann (1833-1897)
Hannah's Girls: Marilla (1851-1916)
Hannah's Girls: Grace (1890-1973)

To order, call 1-800-765-6955.

Visit us at www.reviewandherald.com for information on other Review and Herald® products.

Contents

Introduction

Some years have passed. Grace is married to a minister, Justus Vitrano, and they now live in Milwaukee, Wisconsin.

This fourth book in the *Hannah's Girls* series finds Grace's daughter Ruthie excited about summer vacation. The possibilities for summer fun seem endless. She looks forward to all the adventures she'll have with her best friend, Mary Ann. A trip to Aunt Annie's farm and a visit from her spunky cousin promise excitement too.

But as school starts again a shadow lies over all their lives. There is war in Europe in the actual countries where relatives of Ruthie's classmates are living. Even Ruthie's dad is worried about his family in Sicily.

Even so, school life keeps Ruthie busy. There's recess and games, orchestra practice, a new friend, Esther, and the trial of having that pesky Pearly sit behind her in class.

This true story is Book 4 of a six-book series.

—*Ruth Vitrano Merkel*

Hannah's Girls Family Tree

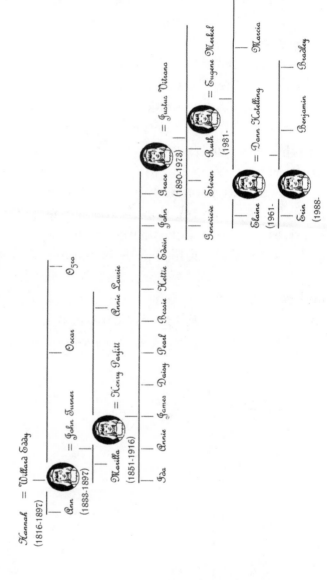

Hannah = Willard Eddy
(1816-1897)

Ann = John Turner
(1838-1897)

Oscar   Ozro

Marilla = Henry Parfitt
(1851-1916)

Ida Annie James Daisy Pearl Bessie Hettie Edwin John Grace = Justus Vittana
                                                          (1890-1928)

Annie Laurie

Genevieve Steven Ruth = Eugene Merkel
                   (1981-)

Marcia

Elaine = Dann Kotelling
(1961-)

Benjamin   Bradley

Erin
(1988-)

Generation Four

Ruthie
(Born 1931)

ERIN'S GRANDMOTHER

Some of the people you'll meet in Ruthie . . .

MARY ANN: Ruthie's best friend.

GEN: Ruthie's big sister. She's 10 years older than Ruthie, and in college.

STEVE: Ruthie's big brother. He's starting college in the fall.

CAROL: Ruthie's cousin who lives on a farm.

AUNT BESSIE AND UNCLE CHARLIE: Ruthie's aunt and uncle. Aunt Bessie is an older sister of Ruthie's mom.

DUTCHIE, GLORIA, BUDDY, AND MAXIE: some of Ruthie's neighborhood friends.

DORIS: one of Ruthie's best school friends.

MR. SANDERS: owns the neighborhood grocery store.

ORRELLA: Ruthie's spunky cousin from Chicago.

LYLA: a nosy classmate.

ESTHER: a shy new classmate.

ONE

Summer Vacation

Ruthie's eyes popped open wide.

Sunlight streamed through her bedroom window, and the white, puffy curtains billowed toward the bed in the early-morning breeze. She looked over at her sister, Genevieve, who still was sound asleep.

Gen had arrived home in the late afternoon just the day before. School was out for her, too. She'd come from Michigan, riding with some of her friends all the way home to Wisconsin. Ruthie felt proud of Gen. She had just finished her first year at Emmanuel Missionary College.

Ruthie was so glad to have her one and only sister home again. Even though there was more than 10 years' difference in their ages, they were very close. Gen always said that Mom and Dad had Ruthie just for her! That admiration went both ways. Ruthie adored her big sister. She thought Gen was wonderful, beautiful, and perfect— even her teeth! It was true, Gen's teeth were straight and even, and Ruthie hoped that when she got all her second teeth they would be just as attractive as Gen's.

She ran her tongue over a certain tooth. It didn't hurt, but it seemed that it could hurt. She pushed it with her tongue. It moved easily. She pressed an experimental finger against it. Ooops, now that did hurt a bit. This tooth had been wiggling around for days, and she thought it was time it came out. "I'll just keep wiggling it," she said very quietly to herself.

It was the first day of summer vacation, and Ruthie loved the warm weather and the months off from school. What would she and her neighborhood friends do today? Play tag, or hide-and-seek, or hopscotch? Maybe someone would think of something else exciting to do. Time would tell. Whatever came to their minds would be fun. It was just too exciting to sleep. Who knew what could happen, especially with Mary Ann around?

Ruthie figured that Gen deserved some extra time to rest after that long trip. But it wasn't that she needed beauty rest. Not at all! With Gen's naturally curly hair and gorgeous sapphire-blue eyes, Ruthie thought she was as pretty as a movie star. Everyone noticed her eyes. Mom said that Gen's eyes were the same color as Grandma Marilla's had been. Ruthie had never met her, because she'd passed away before any of Mom's children were born, but she thought that she must have been pretty too.

Ruthie carefully slid out of bed so that she didn't squeak the springs. She tiptoed to the window, where she could look down to the street below. All was quiet. Was the whole world asleep?

No. She titled her head at the clip-clop of the milkman's horse. He was smart, that horse. He knew just where to stop, whether Ollie, the milkman, told him to or not. Ollie might be held up at a house taking another order. The horse would make his way slowly up the street and stop at the house of their next customer. Ruthie always thought that riding in a wagon to deliver milk would be nice work in the summer but not the winter. Wisconsin winters were brr-r-r cold.

Wish Mary Ann would come along just now, or Dutchie, or Gloria, or Buddy, or Maxie. Wonder what's keeping them all?

Her neighborhood friends were all fun to be with. She had met each one of them on the first day she moved into their house on Hopkins Street. Well, all except Mary Ann, who'd come about a year after Ruthie's family did. Ever since then Mary Ann had been her best neighborhood pal.

Ruthie's family had moved to Milwaukee from Chicago when she was only 4. She didn't remember much about the move, but she surely remembered the city they'd moved from. They still went back to visit family and friends who lived there. Chicago was huge, while Milwaukee was . . . She stopped and glanced out the window again. She couldn't think of a word to describe this city they lived in. Their neighborhood was like a small town. Everyone knew everyone else.

Looking across the street, she saw Mrs. Reagan shaking her throw rugs. She was a very nice woman, but she didn't want kids to run across her lawn. That was certain! Up the street Ollie and his faithful horse were just about out of sight. She looked straight down and saw the petunias and marigolds right against the house in her aunt Bessie's flower beds. In the quiet of the morning she heard her dad running water in the sink to shave. When she was small, she used to like watching him swirl the short, round-bottomed brush in his shaving mug, then lather up his face. Sometimes he'd tease her with a bit of bubbly foam on her nose.

She cocked her head. From downstairs she heard footsteps. That would be either her aunt or her uncle getting dressed for the day. This was a comfortable house. She liked that her aunt and uncle lived downstairs.

What would I call Milwaukee? she thought. Then suddenly she knew, and said the words aloud. "I'd call it home."

Ruthie and her family lived upstairs in a white, two-story house that sat atop a low hill on the corner of Hopkins Street and Auer Avenue. Their second-story home had three bedrooms, a bath, a kitchen, and a dining room and living room combined. Out in the hallway were steps that led either downstairs or upstairs to the attic.

Downstairs, Aunt Bessie lived with her doctor husband, Uncle Charlie. On the first floor was one bedroom, a bath, a tiny kitchen screened off from the dining room, and a living room with a beautiful baby grand piano. The rest of the downstairs area was Uncle Charlie's doctor's office, and it had a waiting room and an office and examination room.

There wasn't much of a yard, but what there was was neat and pretty. Narrow flower beds ran along the edge of the basement wall, and two snowball bushes grew near the front porch. A great old maple tree towered in the corner of the yard.

Mother was Aunt Bessie's youngest sister. They came from a family of 10 children born to Henry and Marilla Parfitt in New London, Wisconsin.

Sitting there at her bedroom window, Ruthie could still remember the day she and her family moved in. It seemed like only yesterday.

Aunt Bessie had run out to welcome everyone, and Uncle Charlie was right beside her. "You're here at last! This is wonderful!" Aunt Bessie had said. Everyone hugged everyone else.

Ruthie knew immediately that she would like her new home. It would be far different from living in Chicago, where the city was bigger and life was busier. She hadn't had an open yard in Chicago, and the houses were closer together. Ruthie's father was a Seventh-day Adventist minister, and he'd had been asked to move to Milwaukee to be the pastor of a church there. So there they were.

Now nearly five years later Ruthie laughed to herself. "Hello, Milwaukee!" she whispered. 🌼

TWO

Uncle Charlie's Pancakes

Ruthie," Gen said with a yawn. "You're up."

Ruthie sank down on the bed with a bounce. "I've been up for hours—well, at least for a while," she told her sister. "It's summer vacation. No telling what might happen today—maybe something exciting."

Gen stretched and yawned again, a loud yawn that ended in a big, long sigh. "You always were one to get up at the crack of dawn," she said groggily. "But I guess I'll get up too. Uncle Charlie is making a pancake breakfast today, remember?" She scooted out of the bed and stretched her arms toward the ceiling while Ruthie looked at her with approval. Ruthie thought Gen was pretty even with her curly hair tumbled from sleep. She turned to look in the mirror at her own straight brown hair, twisting a strand around one finger. She wished it had a wave somewhere, but it didn't.

Mary Ann once said that Ruthie's hair was as straight as a stick, and Ruthie had thought about that for a long time. Most sticks had at least one bump or little curve to them, so that didn't make any sense. With a silly smile at the girl in the mirror, Ruthie slipped off her nightie and into a sundress.

"Beat you to the basement," she called as she grabbed her sandals and ran toward the stairs.

"Don't start breakfast without me!" Gen laughed. "Tell 'em I'm coming."

❧

Once in a while Uncle Charlie made a big stack of pancakes and the two families ate breakfast together. It was fun eating in Aunt Bessie's summer kitchen in the basement. The room was small but cheery, especially when the morning sun peeped in the windows. This morning the table was dressed up with a red-and-white-checkered cloth. They were celebrating Gen's return.

"Well, Steve, did you bring your appetite?" Uncle Charlie teased as he placed a large steaming platter of pancakes on the table. Ruthie's brother, Steve, was a lean young man and growing tall. When school started in September, he would be in college too.

"I brought mine," Ruthie chimed.

"Me too," Gen echoed, sliding onto the last chair.

It only took a minute for the platter to go round the circle, each person forking off two or three or four of the special treat. A tub of delicious Wisconsin butter from Ollie's milk wagon followed the pancakes, and a bottle of syrup after that.

Seven heads bent over the table. Knives and forks clicked. Then Steve looked up. "Can you believe it?" he asked, swallowing his first mouthful. "We forgot to say the blessing."

"Why, you're right. In our haste we forgot to ask the blessing," Aunt Bessie said, stopping her hand halfway to her mouth.

"We're no better than the heathen," Dad said with a smile. The others smiled too. Dad usually made that statement when someone forgot to say grace. Ruthie always got a tickle out of him saying that. She imagined them as people from the Pacific islands that she'd seen on the Sabbath school Picture Roll.

Sheepishly they each put down their utensils. "Let's repeat our family blessing," Mother suggested. Seven heads bowed over their plates, and the family recited:

> "God is great, God is good,
> and we thank Him for this food.
> By His goodness all are fed.
> Give us, Lord, our daily bread. Amen."

"There, now, we can continue!" With a big smile Gen picked up her fork. "We're no longer heathen."

The talk was of summer and vacation, and vegetable gardens and travel. Boring adult talk, but Ruthie was content to listen. She tried to understand why Dad and Uncle Charlie spoke with concern about events taking place overseas in Europe far, far away. There was a bad man named Hitler who was a big worry. He was stirring up trouble all over the place. You often heard his name on the radio and sometimes in newspaper stories that Dad read aloud. His name even came up in bits of conversation that Ruthie overheard in town. Even kids recognized the name Hitler when they heard it.

The platter went around again, as did a plate of cinnamon toast and a bowl of berries.

"Can I have some cinnamon toast, please?" Ruthie asked.

"May I," Gen corrected in a kind voice. Gen planned to be a teacher. She'd decided to be a teacher when she was just 4 years old. Even though Gen corrected Ruthie's grammar Ruthie thought she'd be a good teacher. Gen read all the time and had a large vocabulary. She never missed a chance to tell you that you'd mispronounced or misused a word.

Sometimes Ruthie became exasperated with her sister's guidance, but she guessed it was best. Mother agreed with Gen because she believed people should know how to speak their native language correctly. And besides, Gen's knowledge of the English language and her correct use of words had gotten her a job at college. She was a "reader" for a professor in the English Department. Ruthie thought that was a perfect job for Gen because she was always reading anyway. But Gen had explained that readers read and corrected the papers and tests that the students did for their classes.

So that kind of reader was another new word for Ruthie's vocabulary. ❀

THREE

Forty-eight Memory Verses

"Are you about ready to head to the farm?" Uncle Charlie asked.

Steve took a long swig of milk. "Guess so, in a few days anyway. I'm going to help Dad with his garden until it's time to go. And I'll shoot some baskets with the fellows over on the playground when I'm not working with Dad."

Ruthie let her gaze wander through the window to the small backyard. You'd have a tiny little garden if you put one there! Dad's garden was on the edge of the city in the yard of some friends who had plenty of wide-open space around their house. They were happy for Dad to put in a big garden there. He'd planted a few rows of corn and lots of tomatoes. Then there were rows of peas and green beans. Last were the hills of cucumbers and zucchini. She'd wondered about the "hills" of cukes and zucchini until she found out that Dad had planted the seeds in little piles of heaped-up dirt so that the plants had room to spread out.

Aunt Annie and Uncle Reynolds lived on a farm up near New London, where Mom had lived when she was a girl. Mom and her nine brothers and sisters had been born there. Aunt Annie was second oldest, Aunt Bessie was the sixth child, and Mom, whose name was Grace, was the youngest. Ruthie loved the farm with its big barn, the pastures and meadows, the horses, the milk cows, the cute calves, the chickens, and the geese.

Steve loved it there too. "It's best for a city boy to spend his summers in the country," his parents said many times, and Steve agreed. Summer vacation got boring after just a few days in the city, but there was always something going on at the farm. Steve had learned to pitch hay, drive the horses, and milk the cows. He didn't even mind the big hissing, honking geese. It sort of made him laugh that Ruthie hated them.

Ruthie thought the geese were too bold and bossy, and they plagued her nearly to death pecking at her heels through the open steps of the back porch. Sometimes they'd even follow Ruthie and her cousin Carol, honking and hissing. Carol would turn on them, stamp her foot, and shout, "Go away, you miserable geese!" Then she'd dash toward them, shooing them with a wild wave of her arms. That always did the trick, for the geese would turn and waddle away as fast as they could.

But Ruthie didn't have to worry about them yet. She looked out the basement window, daydreaming of her and Carol having fun. Carol had a bicycle!

Oooh, how Ruthie longed to have a bicycle. She spoke of it often to Mom and Dad, but she understood that times were hard and that there was no extra money for a bike—especially now that there would be two Vitrano children going to college.

"Good breakfast, Charlie," she half heard her dad say to her uncle. "Next time it'll be my turn."

"I can't wait, Justus," Uncle Charlie replied with a grin. "Your spaghetti dinners are the best ever."

And that was true. Dad was a wonderful cook. He'd been born on the island of Sicily and had come to the United States when he was only 16. He loved to cook, and specialized in Italian dishes.

"I'm going to listen to the morning's news report before I start anything else," said Uncle Charlie. He and Dad always shared any news about the trouble overseas. Many German people lived in Milwaukee, and the trouble with Hitler and the Nazi forces in Germany worried many families in the neighborhood. Dad was concerned about his family in Sicily, too.

"Guess I'll check on the news too," Dad told him. "It's hard to understand what's driving that insane Hitler, and Mussolini is no better."

Uncle nodded his head as they headed up the stairs. Mom volunteered Ruthie and Gen to help Aunt Bessie clear the table and wash dishes.

"Girls, please help your aunt with the dishes. I'm taking Steve with me to check on lengthening his work pants. He's grown taller, and I'm going to have to rehem and adjust his trousers before he goes to Aunt Annie's. Bessie, maybe you and I can work on our quilts sometime later in the day."

"Gen," said Ruthie as she put the last of Aunt Bessie's plates on the cupboard shelf, "I have a loose tooth. It's the last of my baby teeth. See?"

"Want me to pull it?" Aunt Bessie asked. She was a nurse and had met Uncle Charlie at Dr. Kellogg's Battle Creek Sanitarium when she was taking nurses' training and Uncle Charlie was taking premed.

"No, I'll do it myself," Ruthie said. And she did right then and there. She just pulled it out with her fingers.

"You rascal, you!" Gen said with a sparkle in her eye. She led Ruthie to the sink, where she gave her a glass of cold water. "You've done a lot of growing since I saw you last."

Ruthie washed a little blood from her mouth with the water. "Well, it's not too hard to pull a tooth. First I make sure it's good and loose and wiggles easy back and forth before I try to pull it." She looked up at her sister with a snaggle-toothed smile.

"You are such a plucky girl," said Aunt Bessie. "Have you thought of becoming a nurse?"

"Nope, I don't think so," Ruthie replied.

"Maybe a doctor? I've noticed how interested you are in looking at Uncle Charlie's glass cabinet in the office, where he keeps his instruments."

"Naw, I don't think I want to be a doctor." Ruthie made a funny face. "I don't like the smell of ether."

Gen laughed and tweaked her little sister's cheek. "Don't worry. There's plenty of time for you to decide what you want to be when you grow up."

Ruthie danced away from her sister's grasp, but Gen

caught the hem of her skirt. "Before you go out to play, why not recite for Aunt Bessie and me the memory verses I hear you've been learning? Mom wrote that you'll be ready to recite 48 on the last Sabbath in December."

"I'd rather go outside to play, but OK, I'll repeat a couple." She thought a moment. "OK. 'Seek ye first the kingdom of God, and his righteousness; and all these things shall be added unto you.' Matthew 6:33. My *favorite* one is Psalm 91:11 and 12. 'He shall give his angels charge over thee, to keep thee in all thy ways. They shall bear thee up in their hands, lest thou dash thy foot against a stone.'"

She looked at Aunt Bessie with a smile. "I think of that picture you have hanging in your dining room, of the angel watching over two children who are playing near a stream. I like that picture."

Gen smiled proudly at her sister, and Aunt Bessie touched her eyes with the edge of her apron. "Uncle Charlie says you have a bright mind, Ruthie, and he doesn't say that about too many children he knows. You'll always be glad you learned these Bible verses, and memorization actually improves your memory, so that's an extra bonus." Aunt Bessie gave Ruthie a squeeze. "Now go play."

"It just takes tenacity," Gen told her aunt.

Ruthie stopped in midstep. "What's tenacity?" she asked, curious about yet another new word from Gen.

"It means perseverance or stick-to-itiveness," Gen explained.

"Oh," Ruthie replied thoughtfully. "Guess I'll have to add that word to my list of big ones."

FOUR

The Kids on Hopkins Street

 Ruthie took the stairs with a hop and a jump and went out to the yard and the big old maple tree. She easily climbed to her favorite limb, which swung out over the sidewalk a bit, and settled back. This was her palace, her throne room. Here she could play that she was a queen and give orders to her servants.

From her perch in the tree she could look uphill to Townsend Street and downhill almost to the drugstore on 20th Street. That's where she and Mary Ann bought ice-cream cones—if and when they had the money to do so. It cost a whole nickel to get two scoops—and how Ruthie loved chocolate ice cream. She smacked her lips just thinking about it. Mary Ann usually got butter pecan.

As she gazed about the familiar scene she thought of the last time Steve had raced with the Number 12 streetcar on Hopkins Street. He loved to sleep in. Mother always called him in plenty of time to catch the streetcar so that he'd get to school on time. But he just could not make himself roll out of bed at Mom's first call.

That particular day Ruthie had called to him, "Hurry

up, Steve! The streetcar has stopped at Townsend Street. I see people getting off and on. Hurry!"

The next stop would be 20th Street at the drugstore corner. Then the trolley would turn, and Steve would have no way to catch it.

Steve had bolted out of his room, raced through the kitchen, and grabbed the lunch bag that Mom had placed on the kitchen table. He tore down the steps just in time to see the streetcar rolling past on its way down the hill. Steve dashed across the street and bolted down Hopkins Street right behind the streetcar. Just as the conductor clanged the bell before takeoff, Steve jumped aboard through the back door.

"Hurray!" Ruthie remembered her cheer. "He made it again!" It was exciting to see Steve do his Olympic chase.

But Mother had wagged her head and, taking a deep breath, said in a voice of mock despair, "He'll be the death of me yet!"

Dad had been at his desk working on a sermon. He'd looked out the window and seen the entire episode. "Your son is a procrastinator when it comes to getting up in the morning!" he'd told Mom.

Mother had smiled. "My son? He's yours, too, you know." And they'd both laughed in relief that Steve had made it through the trolley's back door.

Now Ruthie turned herself to look toward Townsend Street. She wondered what might be going on there. None of her neighborhood friends ever played with the kids in that area. Everyone knew that some real tough boys lived there. Not all of them, of course, but some of the guys had given Townsend Street a rough and rowdy reputation. Ruthie didn't even like walking by there. It just plain scared her.

"I hope I never get involved with the Townsend boys," she said to herself.

Wish Mary Ann would come out. Wonder what she's doing. Mary Ann lived down the street at the opposite corner from Ruthie's house. Ooooh, could Mary Ann tell a story! The biggest stories you ever heard. She loved to play queen, too. She and Ruthie divided up the world, each ruling half. Ruthie was Queen Catherine, and Mary Ann was Queen Victoria.

Mary Ann also loved to sing. Her sweet soprano voice blended well with Ruthie's alto. Since Mary Ann was slightly younger than Ruthie, they weren't in the same classroom at the big Auer Avenue Public School a couple blocks away. Their mothers laughingly figured it was probably best that they weren't—for the good of both the teachers and the girls.

Ruthie sighed. Where was everybody? She was not a girl who sulked or was disagreeable, but she felt a little grouchy that not one of her friends was out and about. She wanted to play with any or all of them—Gloria, Dutchie, Buddy, and Maxie. And, of course, Mary Ann.

Gloria was about three years older than Ruthie. Now that her mother had just had a baby—cute little Judy—

Gloria didn't play as much as she had before. She helped her mom a lot. Playing hopscotch just wasn't the same without Gloria.

Dutchie was Gloria's brother. He liked playing cops and robbers or cowboys and Indians, just running around and chasing imaginary enemies. He and Gloria went to St. Leo's, the Catholic elementary school. Summertime and after school was the time Ruthie played with these pals.

Buddy lived across the street next to Mrs. Reagan. He was very smart and full of information about almost anything. You could bank on it that Buddy would know the answer to almost any question you might have. His smartness didn't make him boring, just interesting. Ruthie laughed to herself, thinking about Buddy. Dad once said that he was a corker! But that was sort of a compliment. Buddy went to the Lutheran elementary school about a mile away, so he wasn't in school with Ruthie and Mary Ann either.

Maxie was the youngest of all the kids in the neighborhood. He was a quiet boy with dark-brown, thoughtful eyes. He was courteous and well-behaved, too. His parents were from Germany, and they'd moved to Milwaukee just before Maxie had been born.

Maxie was . . . well, Maxie was *affable*. That's what Gen had said about him. There was another big word. Gen explained that it meant Maxie was easygoing and fun to be around. She said that people who were affable were always welcome in the circle of friends. Ruthie saw him at school and recess time, but because he was a whole year younger than she was, he was never in her classroom.

Sitting there in the tree, Ruthie drew a deep breath. "Well, now's as good a time as any to practice my memory verses," she told herself. She rattled off the first dozen and a half or so, remembering to repeat the text. Then she slowed down a bit. She knew the more recent ones very well, but she always tried going over the older ones to keep them fresh in her mind. The Thirteenth Sabbath in December seemed a long way off, but she knew she needed to keep up with the memorization and not get behind. Often just as she was drifting off to sleep she'd say a memory verse or two. She liked the warm, peaceful feeling that saying them gave her.

Steve came out, looked up in the maple tree, and waved.

"Where ya goin', Steve?" Ruthie called down to him.

"I'm heading to the playground. Dad said I might as well go shoot some baskets. Before he goes out to the garden he's going to the hospital and visit Paul for a bit."

"Why's Paul in the hospital?"

"He had an emergency appendectomy the other day, remember?"

"Oh, yeah. Is he OK?"

"Think so, but Dad thought he'd better go this morning. While he's out he'll get a new hoe. The other one's broken beyond repair. See ya later!" And Steve was off.

Ruthie remembered how Dad had scowled at the old

hoe the other day. He had tried to fix the handle, but it was no use. Last year he'd replaced the handle with an old broomstick, and now it had broken off. Nothing that was usable got thrown away.

Poor Paul, Ruthie thought. *He got so sick so fast and almost died. I'd rather have my tonsils taken out. No, I'd rather not have that done either. I'm glad my tonsils are gone, thanks to Uncle Charlie.*

Ruthie watched Steve until he crossed Hopkins Street and went into Saunders Market, the neighborhood grocery store. The owner was a friendly fellow, and everybody liked him. He sold vegetables, fruit, a variety of fresh and packaged meats, butter, milk and eggs, canned goods, soaps, brooms, and mops—everything that folks needed.

Steve's friend Hank often worked there part-time. He helped stock the shelves, and he washed the big front windows or swept the wooden floor. He did all the kind of odd jobs that boys could do. Everyone worked these days to make ends meet, especially energetic boys. Mr. Saunders would have liked for Steve to work there too, and Steve wouldn't have minded doing so. But Mom and Dad felt that Steve was better off spending his summers on Aunt Annie's farm, learning to do farm chores and getting tons of fresh air.

"Steve probably went in to say hi to Hank," Ruthie told herself.

After Gen had finished straightening the bedroom

and vacuuming the living room carpet, she came out to look for Ruthie. She wasn't hard to find, for Gen knew how much she loved the big maple tree.

Gen stopped under the tree and looked up at her sister's swinging legs. "Ruthie, you want to walk to the library with me?" she asked.

The legs stopped swinging. "Naw, I want to wait for Mary Ann."

"OK." With a wave Gen was off. She loved books, and there was a small but nice public library about a mile and a half away. All the librarians knew Gen. They remembered her from high school. They also knew that she was in college studying to become a teacher.

Ruthie barely noticed when Dad came out and got in his car.

Ruthie squinted up at the blue sky overhead. Sunbeams slipped through the branches, making magical rays of light, and she basked with pleasure in their warmth. The leaves of the tree provided a protective, sheltering cover and partially hid her from view.

"There's sunshine in my soul today," she hummed to herself.

Then Ruthie began singing out loud—anything to while away the time.

> "O I wish I were a gingerbread man with currants on my vest.
> If I'd get hungry I would eat a few of them and then save all the rest.

I'd lean upon a peppermint cane while walking down the street.
If I should see a nice and shiny frosted cake,
that's where I'd take my seat."

Grinning, she remembered her classmate Robby
pulling at the buttons on his shirt and tossing make-be-
lieve currants into his mouth when they sang that song.
He was full of fun, but he was no dummy. Ruthie had to
scurry to keep ahead of him in her grades. She usually got
the best of him, but he gave her a run for her money.
Robby lived way on the other side of the school, so she
never saw him in the summer.

The mailman walked by with his leather bag slung
over his shoulder. He whistled a little tune as he delivered
mail to each house. Ruthie was quiet as a mouse, and the
mailman did not notice her up on her perch—her throne.
He dropped a couple letters in the family mailbox, which
hung to the side of the doorframe.

*Right where they hung the quarantine sign when I had
chicken pox,* Ruthie thought. The public health nurse had
stopped by and nailed the sign to the house. She let her
legs swing again, musing and daydreaming. She thought
of how she'd had to stay in the house. Her classmates had
not been allowed to come and visit, even though she'd
not been very sick at all. *Glad I'm not sick very much. I
haven't missed a day of school except for the times we go up to
see Aunt Annie.*

FIVE

Buddy Gets a Bike

 Suddenly—finally—Ruthie heard a familiar voice. "Good morning, Your Royal Highness. How are you today, Queen Catherine?"

It was Mary Ann squinting up at her with a grin.

In a very prim and proper manner Ruthie playfully replied, "And good morning to you, Queen Victoria. You are looking well today. What have you planned for us to do? Shall we inspect the royal flower gardens?"

As she talked, Ruthie was climbing down from her lofty roost. "I wondered where you were and why you hadn't come outside to play," she told her friend.

"Oh, I was visiting with my aunt Effie and uncle Hale," Mary Ann said. "You remember them. They're here at our house for a day or two; then they'll go back home to Sheboygan." She said the tongue-twister town name perfectly. "So Mom wanted me to take my time at breakfast and not run off real fast. I didn't mind eating slow anyhow, 'cause uncle Hale is such fun!"

Ruthie nodded. "I remember your uncle Hale. He's nice. Remember when he told us how the town of Sheboygan got its name?"

"Do I ever!" Mary Ann giggled.

Uncle Hale had explained that a long time ago a settler and his family lived in the area that is now Sheboygan. Their closest neighbors were a young Indian man and his wife and three boys. Then the settlers heard that the Indian woman was going to have another baby, and that the whole family hoped it would be a girl baby. However, when the baby came, the Indian dad told the settler that they'd another son. "She-boy-again" was how he explained it.

"And," Uncle Hale told the girls, "that's how the town got its name!"

Both Mary Ann and Ruthie had giggled and giggled at that. Of course, they could tell by the twinkle in uncle Hale's eye that it was just a tall tale. It did make a good story, though, and the girls still had fun laughing at the joke. But now Mary Ann changed the subject.

"I have a plan for us, Ruthie. We're going to do something really unusual this summer," she said. She drew out the words, making it sound mysterious.

"Good. I'm ready for some fun," Ruthie said happily. No telling what it was, but that's one thing that made Mary Ann exciting. She had so many ideas.

"Yep," Mary Ann said with a nod. "After talking with Aunt Effie this morning, I have decided that you and I will take a walk in the cemetery." She looked at Ruthie to see her reaction, and she was not disappointed.

"What?" Ruthie exclaimed. "A walk in the cemetery? I've heard of a walk on the beach or in the park, but never a walk in the cemetery!"

"Now you've heard it," Mary Ann teased. "Aunt Effie was telling me about a man and woman who are buried there, and I want to see their tombstones."

Ruthie's big eyes said it all. Mary Ann had come up with some wild things, but this topped everything.

Mary Ann's family lived right across the street from Union Cemetery, but the girls had never ventured far inside. It was huge, and enclosed by a tall chain-link fence. The grounds were always kept up neatly, and with its many lovely trees and bushes it looked like a beautiful park.

Ruthie spun around on one foot. "Whenever you're ready, I am," she declared. "But I hope it's in the next day or two—before we go to my aunt Annie's farm." Ruthie didn't want anything to interfere with her trip to the farm.

Mary Ann linked her arm through Ruthie's. "Then we'll have to make sure we do it soon. But for now," she giggled, "I almost forgot. Mom gave me money to get a pound of butter at Mr. Saunders'."

"Well, then, let's go. Maybe he'll give us a treat!"

Looking each way before they stepped from the curb, the girls ran across Hopkins Street and pulled open Mr. Saunders' squeaky screen door. It slammed shut behind them with a bang.

Mr. Saunders stood behind his bright new slicing machine, cutting his delicious Wisconsin orange cheddar cheese. Hank, his helper, stood on a ladder stocking canned goods on the shelves.

"Hi, Mr. Saunders," the girls called. The grocer wore a long white apron over his blue-checkered shirt and black pants. His bald head was as shiny as his eyes. He stopped what he was doing and walked over to meet the girls.

"Well, if it isn't my favorite royal princesses," he said with a bow. "What are you up to today? Will there be any executions, or will it be an arrest of a swindler at the street bazaar?" He well knew of the girls' escapades, and he enjoyed playing along.

Mary Ann held up her hand and corrected Mr. Saunders. "Excuse me, sir, but we are queens. Not princesses." She lifted her chin and announced, "Today we are going to take the royal yacht for a cruise down the Regal River." Giggling, she asked, "Wanna come along?"

He shook his head sadly. "I guess not. My master, Hank, won't let me off today."

Hank grinned and nodded.

Mr. Saunders stepped to the block of cheese and cut off two small corners, then handed them to his young guests. They politely thanked him and quickly popped the cheese into their mouths.

When she had swallowed her treat, Mary Ann said, "My mother would like a pound of butter, please. Here's the money." She plunked down the coins on the tall countertop.

"Coming right up, ma'am. And while you're here, take your time and look around. I've got some new red licorice sticks in this morning."

Mary Ann's eyes grew bright as she stepped toward the candy counter. But Ruthie checked out the gumball machine with its shiny, round globe top. She liked looking at the different-colored small, round gumballs inside. If she ever had a penny, it was spent on the gumball machine. That was certain.

"Say there, Ruthie, you're getting right good at roller skating," Mr. Saunders told her. "I saw you practicing your turns the other day. You flew around and headed in the opposite direction real fast and neat." He handed Mary Ann the wrapped pound of butter.

"Well," Ruthie said, dragging her eyes from the red and blue and yellow gumballs, "my sister told me some time back that I should hold one foot steady and turn with the other. It's faster that way. It works with ice skating, too."

Then the girls said, "Thank you," waved, and left the store.

Hank and Mr. Saunders rolled their eyes at each other. Those two were quite a pair, and their shenanigans always provided amusement.

"Ain't they somethin'!" Hank laughed. "Sometimes I see them walkin' half bent over. Looks crazy, but they're laughin' and talkin' the whole time."

"Yeah, that's their dungeon walk, they tell me. It seems some enemy has captured them and they're doing a forced march. My little daughter, Gwen, wishes she lived here in the store so she could be with Ruthie and Mary Ann all day, every day."

"Well," said Mary Ann as the girls left the store, "we'd better hurry to my house and give this butter to my mother before it gets soft. Then you can see Uncle Hale again."

Uncle Hale met them at the door. "How ya doin', Ruthie? Haven't seen you in a coon's age," he said, opening the screen door for both girls to come in.

Ruthie stood politely just inside the door, not venturing into the house. Mary Ann had run to the kitchen and given the butter to her mother. Then she ran back to Ruthie. But before they could run off to play, Uncle Hale held up his hand.

"Wait a minute, young ladies; I've got a question for you." His eyes sparkled, and he had a sly smile on his face.

The girls grinned at each other. Uncle Hale was always fun.

"There were five birds sitting on a wire," he said. "I shot one. How many were left?"

"Four," they replied as they turned to open the door.

"Nope; you're both wrong!" he boomed.

They looked at each other. What now?

So Mary Ann summed it up. "Five minus one is four, Uncle Hale." She shook her finger at him. "Have you forgotten?"

He shook *his* head. "Nope. And I tell you, you are wrong—dead wrong."

The girls looked at each other again. Ruthie giggled. "OK, how many were left?" she asked.

"None. The others all flew away," Uncle Hale said with a chuckle.

The girls groaned and rolled their eyes. "Oh, Uncle Hale," Mary Ann laughed.

"You girls run on and have fun now," her uncle told them.

They skipped down the steps to the sidewalk, and continued as they went up the street. "I'll bet the kids all liked Uncle Hale when he was a kid in school," said Ruthie. "Gen still laughs when she thinks about him telling us that the song 'Hail, Hail, the Gang's All Here' was written about him."

Down the street in front of Ruthie's house they saw Buddy, Dutchie, and Maxie all waiting for them.

"Hi!" they yelled in chorus.

It was then that Ruthie saw that the boys were standing in front of a small bicycle.

"What's this?" she asked, running toward Buddy. He'd said that his grandpa was looking for a sidewalk bike for him. It looked as though he'd found one.

"Oh, Buddy, a bicycle! You are so lucky."

Ruthie walked round and round the bike, giving it a thorough inspection.

"His grandpa found it for sale at the Goodwill store. So he bought it and cleaned it up," Dutchie told her.

"That's right," Buddy nodded. "He just brought it over this morning. That's why I didn't come out sooner. I visited with Grandpa until he left."

Ruthie's heart skipped a beat. "Buddy, you are the luckiest boy in the world."

"Yeah," said the other kids. "He sure is."

"Will you let us ride it?" Dutchie asked. He wanted a bike of his own too.

"Sure," Buddy said cheerfully. His blue eyes twinkled. "I will if you'll give me a baseball card once in a while."

Baseball cards came with packages of bubble gum. On each card was a picture of a major-league baseball player and information about him. Buddy had quite a collection of cards, and how he loved to show them to everyone. He faithfully listened to baseball games on the radio and knew each team's standing. If anyone wanted to know anything about baseball, Buddy was the one to ask.

"You sure are lucky, Buddy," Maxie said.

A bicycle, thought Ruthie. *Will I ever get one? I want a bike so much. But I know we can't afford one with Gen and Steve both being in college next year. Well, I'll just have to start praying for a miracle.* Ruthie was dead serious. She believed that Jesus heard children's prayers.

"Buddy, when I get a bike of my own, I'll be sure to give you as many rides as you want," she promised. She felt confident that her prayer would be answered.

He nodded his head and said with a grin, "OK, I'll remember."

Then Buddy asked Ruthie if she wanted a ride. "Oh, yes!" she told him. She'd never ridden a two-wheeler before, but she was ready to try. She got on while Buddy held the back wheel. She pushed down on the pedals, and Buddy let go. She rode a few feet; the bike wobbled and stopped a couple times.

Buddy came to help. "Turn the wheel in the direction you think you are going to fall, and that will rescue you," he explained, and sure enough, it worked. She got the hang of it and rode down to the corner, turned around, and came back. Mary Ann did the same thing.

Just then Maxie's mother called him. "Moxie, Moxie!"

"Wonder what she wants," Maxie said as he jumped up and headed for home.

"It always sounds strange to hear his mother say his name so funny," said Ruthie as she watched him go.

"Yeah," agreed Buddy, "but that's her German accent. My mom says they must be very glad to be here in America with all that trouble going on where they used to live in Stuttgart, Germany."

Mary Ann nodded her agreement. "My uncle still lives over there in Berlin, and my folks are worried for him."

"That Hitler man is a tyrant," Dutchie chimed in. "My dad says he's bound for trouble."

They all sat quietly for a bit, thinking about the possibility of war. They couldn't comprehend just what war would be like, but they knew it was terrible. However, Germany was far away, so they didn't give it deep thought. The conversations they overheard just lingered in the back of their minds. You couldn't get away from it these days.

Buddy and Dutchie took off to do something else, so Ruthie and Mary Ann decided to roller-skate. After they'd put their skates on over their shoes and turned the key to lock them firmly in place, they took off and sailed down to the corner. There they turned around. Back and forth they went, Ruthie showing Mary Ann how to make a wide circle with only one foot whenever they turned.

Mr. Jensen, an old retired neighbor, was sitting on his

porch in an old rocking chair. He waved at them each time they passed his house. He had to walk with a cane, so they rarely saw him out and about.

"My folks have known Mr. and Mrs. Jensen for ages," Mary Ann said, finally stopping to catch her breath. "They all used to live in Wauwatosa. It's a . . . it's a coincidence that we live near each other again." She spun in a wide circle. "Is *coincidence* the right word?" she asked.

"I think so," Ruthie said. "My aunt Bessie calls him a kind old gent. *Gent* is a funny word too." The girls giggled.

Ruthie turned her head just in time to see Steve coming down the street holding a handkerchief to his chin.

"What happened, Steve?" Ruthie asked with a little squeal. Suddenly there was a funny feeling in her chest. Was he bleeding?

"Oh, I tripped on a little kid's shoe someone left lying on the basketball court" was his muffled reply. "I fell and hit my chin."

With a quick "I gotta go" to Mary Ann, Ruthie hurried after her brother. Her heart beat hard with worry.

Ruthie skated into the grass, quickly slipped out of her skates, and went into the house. She was just in time to hear Mom tell Steve to go right down to Uncle Charlie.

Ruthie felt as if her heart was going to stop as he hurried by her. She saw red spots on the handkerchief he still held to his chin. Her beloved brother was hurt. Now what? She could smell Mom's good cream of tomato soup cooking, but she did not feel like eating. She just stood there wringing her hands.

"He'll be fine. Don't worry," Mom said, drawing her little girl into a protective hug.

Mother was always a source of encouragement. She knew how to judge such things. After all, she was the mother of three children.

Years back Mom had lived with Aunt Bessie and Uncle Charlie. That was after her own mother had died and she no longer needed to stay in New London to take care of her. So Mom had jumped at the chance to come and live with her sister and go to business college. Of course, she wasn't Mom then. Back then she was only Grace. And to pay for her board and room Grace had helped her sister Bessie take care of *her* three children— John, Helen, and Maynard.

Way back then Aunt Bessie and Uncle Charlie had trained Mom to help in the medical office that they had in the front part of their house. (By that time Uncle Charlie had become a doctor and Aunt Bessie was his nurse.) Mom even learned to help give anesthesia. So Ruthie understood that her mother knew about taking care of sick and hurt people. If she said that Steve would be OK, Ruthie believed her. But it still hurt her to see him hurt.

It wasn't too long before Steve came up the stairs. He had a bandage on his chin. Mom fussed over him a little and made him lie down for a spell.

Steve said that he really was OK. However, he did sprawl out on the sofa and then told them what was under that bandage. After Uncle Charlie had cleaned the wound, he had closed the cut with three small stitches.

"With no anesthesia?" asked Ruthie with wide eyes. She knew the smell of ether in the hallway when Uncle Charlie did some minor surgery or a tonsillectomy, and she had not noticed that familiar odor.

"None whatsoever." He winked at his younger sister. "But I clutched the sides of the examination table until my knuckles were white. I'm pretty sure of that."

Gen walked in, and Dad arrived almost on her heels. So Steve had to tell the story of his fall all over again. Dad immediately knelt down on a knee to get a good view of the bandage. Then he placed his hand on Steve's.

"Thank God that it was no worse," he said quietly. He gently pushed Steve's hair from his forehead, then smiled and stood up.

Gen shivered. She too was tenderhearted.

"I'm sure you gritted your teeth when Uncle stitched that cut," Gen told him. "I know I would have. Wow, no anesthesia!"

Ruth's young heart swelled with both pride and sympathy for her courageous brother. When he got up and sat in the big rocking chair, she sat on the stool next to him and held his hand. He grinned at her and winked again.

Gen brought Steve his soup and salad on a tray. Oh yes, he was treated royally.

"Uncle Charlie told me my chin will heal quickly. The scar won't be large at all," Steve added. "He doesn't think it will even be noticeable."

"He's a good doctor," agreed Mother.

The next day dawned sunny and warm—just perfect, the girls agreed—for a walk in the cemetery. Ruthie reminded her mom that she'd said they could go, and turned to skip down the stairs.

"Just a moment, Ruthie. Wait," Mother called.

Ruthie turned and came back. "You said . . . ," she began.

"Yes, of course," Mom agreed with a smile. "But before you and Mary Ann go, I want to remind you of something."

Ruthie sank into a kitchen chair, and Mom dried her hands on a tea towel and sat next to her. "Please remember, Ruthie, that you're going to a cemetery, not a playground."

"I know that," Ruthie said, a little puzzled.

"Your behavior in a cemetery should be respectful and proper," Mom said solemnly. "You girls are going there to have fun, and that's OK. But there could be a funeral nearby. There might be a family who is grieving the loss of a loved one."

Ruthie nodded.

"Do you remember when your dad conducted a graveside ceremony for Lucy's grandmother and how sad we all felt?" Mom asked her.

"Yes." And she did remember. Lucy had felt so sad, and her heart had hurt with Lucy.

"Well, let your actions be such that no one is offended. Agreed?"

"I will. I promise," Ruthie told her with a nod.

Mother patted her daughter's head, then cupped her chin in her hand with a smile. "I'm sure Mary Ann's mother is telling her the same thing."

"You needn't worry about us, Mama." She stood and gave her a hug. "We'll behave. We'll be 'proper English ladies' just like Aunt Bessie says."

With that she skipped down the stairs and out the door, and took off for her best friend's house. It was a warm, wonderful day. Suddenly she giggled. She was remembering the afternoon she and Gen had stretched out on their bed after drinking some lemonade Aunt Bessie had made. Aunt Bessie had said something about doing things properly, and Gen had chuckled. "Oh yes, Aunt Bessie," she'd said solemnly, "we are proper English young ladies."

Ruthie had giggled too. "We're proper, all right. Mom and Dad see to that!"

Gen had nodded as she looked up at the ceiling. "We're proper English young ladies, with inherited Irish humor and lighthearted, cheerful Italian love of music and beauty! Mix that all together, and you know what you get?"

"What?" Ruthie had asked.

"Genevieve, Steven, and Ruth!"

How they'd laughed at that!

Minutes later Ruthie and Mary Ann skipped down to the gate guarding the entrance to Union Cemetery. This was not the main entrance used by cars, but just a nice paved walk for people who wanted to come in. After only the tiniest pause, they walked on in.

"How will we find these graves?" Ruthie asked after they'd gone a few yards.

"Aunt Effie said to follow the lane to the road, then follow the road until it makes a fork," Mary Ann explained.

So off they went. At the fork they turned left, and sure enough, in just a few minutes they saw a slight hill ahead. As they drew closer they could see two large tombstones.

"My stars!" said Ruthie in surprise. "I've never seen anything like this."

Both girls stood stock-still and gazed at the two huge tombstones. Each was shaped like a coffin with the departed one in full size lying on top of it.

"Careful. Don't step on the graves," Ruthie cautioned as they slowly went closer.

"Well, I never," Mary Ann said quietly. She looked at Ruthie. Her eyes were like saucers.

"This is unbelievable," Ruthie whispered. "This reminds me of an open casket at a funeral—where you can see the person who has died."

For the first few moments they just stood and looked. Then as the novelty and shock began to wear off, they carefully circled around to the opposite side of the tombstones.

Mary Ann spoke first. "From the looks of things, she was a very plain woman who did not dress with any style."

Ruthie could hear the slightest bit of humor in her friend's voice. "How's that?" she asked.

"Well," said Mary Ann in a loud whisper, "she has no lace collar or pearl buttons on her dress. Compare her to her husband, who is wearing a vest and tie with his suit. Certainly he had good taste and knew how to dress. He probably wasn't a 'dandy,' but he was a step up from his wife."

Ruthie pressed back a giggle with a hand over her mouth. They were careful not to laugh loudly. Across the way and down six or seven rows, people were placing flowers on a grave. And in the other direction one of the grounds caretakers bent over to pull weeds, then tossed them into a small wheelbarrow.

The girls looked at each other. They must behave properly.

"Mary Ann," Ruthie said thoughtfully, "you can't expect the carver to get real fussy and chisel in buttons and bows, can you?"

"No, I suppose not. You're right," she replied.

The girls circled around again, and read the names engraved into stone—"Cordelia Rose Helmer" and "Otto Helmer."

"Their last name doesn't quite fit, does it?" Mary Ann looked at Ruthie with bright eyes and a wide grin. "Instead of Helmer, it should be . . ." She gasped, then got control of herself. "It should be Rocky."

Ruthie grabbed Mary Ann's hand and pulled her along as she walked off. "Better yet, 'Rockefeller'!" Her shoulders shook with laughter. When they were out of earshot from anyone, they did laugh—but quietly.

"Oh, Mary Ann, you are so funny. Just like your uncle Hale!" Ruthie told her. "I wonder what the kids at school will say when I tell them about this."

"They'll think you're pulling their leg. But I'll vouch for you," Mary Ann smiled.

They were still quietly laughing as they headed for

home. Nothing could ever compare to this adventure—not in a lifetime!

That evening at supper Ruthie told about their walk in the cemetery. Everyone was smiling at what Mary Ann said. Then in the sudden quiet Gen added, "Or their names could have been 'Stonebury,' like the town in Massachusetts."

Everyone groaned, and Dad almost choked on his mouthful of food. When he quit coughing, he patted Gen's shoulder. "That was a good one, my girl."

SIX

Riddles and Songs

Two weeks later Steve had his stitches out, and the cut didn't look bad at all. So Dad announced that they'd be making the trip to Aunt Annie's the very next day.

"Tomorrow's Wednesday," he pointed out. "We can stay and visit on Thursday and drive home on Friday. That will get me back here for Sabbath." Ruthie grabbed Dad's hand and jumped up and down with excitement. She understood that they couldn't stay longer, for Dad had to preach on Sabbath. But even one day with her cousins made her very happy.

"I'll see Carol, I'll see Carol," she sang in a little silly voice. "Goody, goody, goody! Carol, Ginny, and Dickie!"

The next morning Ruthie awoke to hear Mom and Steve talking quietly in the kitchen. "Did you remember to pack your Sabbath shirt and tie?" Mom was asking.

Oh, wow! How could I have slept so long? Ruthie had thought she'd be up before dawn. She felt too excited to eat, but Mom insisted that she sit at the table. There was no sense waiting in the car while the family had their breakfast. Before long she felt like having a piece of toast with peanut butter and honey. Then she had homemade applesauce and part of an egg. Still, she bounced up and sideways in her chair until Steve called her a wiggle worm.

There was the hurry to check for last-minute things and to get Steve's suitcase into the car. But soon they were on the road out of Milwaukee and traveling north. The trip usually took about two hours. And even though she loved going to New London, Ruthie always got bored during the trip. So Gen and Steve played alphabet with her, watching every sign along the way in an attempt to be the first to have seen every letter of the alphabet. The rules of the game said that the letters had to be seen in order. You couldn't jump ahead from a "j" to an "m."

They also watched for Burma Shave signs along the road and read every one of them out loud.

Each Burma Shave sign had just two or three words on it and the signs were placed along the road several yards apart. You had to watch carefully to read each sign. All together they made funny rhymes. Their favorite was:

She kissed . . . the hairbrush . . . by mistake . . .
She thought . . . it was her . . . husband, Jake.
Burma Shave

How they all howled with laughter at that one.

Of course, Gen usually brought along a book or two. But today she pulled out a letter she'd received from her friend Liz in Chicago. "Want to hear something clever?" she asked Ruthie. "This will tickle your funny bone."

Naturally, Ruthie was interested. "Sure. Whatcha got,

Gen?" She leaned over and tried to peer at the letter.

"No fair peeking," Gen told her, turning so her sister couldn't read the writing. "Liz sent some riddles, and they're a scream. You'll love them. I saved her letter so that I could read these to you on this trip. Are you ready?"

"Oh, I love riddles," Ruthie squealed. "Ask me!"

"If a rooster laid an egg on the top of a hill, on which side of the hill would the egg roll down?" Gen asked.

Even Mom and Dad looked baffled at that. "Say that again, Gen," Steve told her.

Gen reread the riddle.

Ruthie's face was screwed up in concentration. She could see the chicken in her mind, but she couldn't figure out what way its egg would roll.

"Give up?" Gen asked a moment later.

"Yeah," they all agreed.

"Neither!" Gen laughed. "Roosters don't lay eggs."

"Oh, *brother*," Steve sputtered. "That was a tricky one."

"Read us more!" Ruthie called out.

"OK, here's another one. Does England have a fourth of July?"

"No!" came the answer from several voices. "That one isn't hard to figure out," Steve added. "We beat the British!" His smile was confident.

"You're wrong!" Gen laughed. "Of course they have a fourth of July—the fourth day of July. They just don't celebrate it."

How everyone moaned at that. Sure enough, they realized, July 4 was on all calendars, all over the world.

"OK, what's round on both ends and high in the middle?" Gen asked.

"Oh, I know that one. It's Ohio," Ruthie answered. "I heard that one at school. Robby asked us that one day."

Gen wasn't through yet. "Here's a Bible riddle. Who was the straightest man in the entire Bible?" Gen started to giggle to herself before she could get all the words out.

Turning to each other with puzzled looks, they all shrugged their shoulders helplessly.

"It's Joseph."

"Huh? What?" Dad asked.

"It's Joseph," Gen repeated. "The Bible says that Pharaoh made a ruler out of him," she explained with a giggle.

Everyone but Gen moaned.

"And here's another one," Gen said. "What man in the Bible had no parents?"

Silence.

"Joshua, son of Nun."

That one brought the house down. Dad slapped the steering wheel, he laughed so hard.

To while away some more of the time, the family sang. Mom had helped her children learn to sing harmony while they were very young. "Use your ears," she'd say. First she'd have them sing the melody, and she'd sing alto. Then she'd take the lead and encourage them to harmonize with her. It worked! Later she taught each of them to read notes.

With their dad being a pastor, the children almost grew up in church. Music was a vital part of worship for them, and also a vital part of their lives. Dad had a strong, clear tenor voice. Almost every year he was asked to sing a solo at camp meeting. Ruthie loved it when he sang "The Holy City."

So as they traveled they sang old songs and hymns. They sang patriotic tunes. They sang whatever came to their minds. Ruthie liked it best when they did funny songs such as "Old MacDonald Had a Farm." One of her favorites was sung to the tune of "Battle Hymn of the Republic."

"It isn't any trouble just to s ‑ m ‑ i ‑ l ‑ e.
It isn't any trouble just to s ‑ m ‑ i ‑ l ‑ e.
So smile when you're in trouble,
It will vanish like a bubble,
If you'll only take the trouble just to s ‑ m ‑ i ‑ l ‑ e."

Sometimes they would sing the song several times, adding l ‑ a ‑ u ‑ g ‑ h or g ‑ r ‑ i‑ n. Whatever words they sang, it was a peppy song.

The miles rolled by. It wasn't that the trip was terribly long; it was just—well, not really boring. Ruthie squirmed, trying to think of the right word. Gen would know, but she didn't want to ask her. The trip was—humdrum. That was it. And Ruthie felt that she could even put up with boring, knowing the fun she'd have at the end.

She didn't even mind riding along in silence. It was a comfortable silence as she watched the scenery that seemed to glide by. Ruthie loved the countryside. She liked the fields of corn, and woods, and red barns, and silos. The cows grazing in the meadows were picturesque and peaceful. You didn't see this type of scenery in the city. The city was full of streets that were filled with cars and buses and streetcars. And then there were the houses and tall buildings and lots of people.

Riding along, Ruthie felt a sort of calm awareness that she knew and saw things that not all of her playmates and schoolmates knew or saw. She even recognized the types of cows they passed—brown-spotted Guernsey cows, black-spotted Holsteins, and the smaller all-brown Jerseys. They were the ones with the richest milk.

The warm breeze coming through the windows felt good on Ruthie's face. She drew a deep breath and relaxed, resting her head on Gen's shoulder.

Ooops! There was the huge ski jump off to the side of the highway, on the very top of a giant hill. She didn't want to miss seeing that. In the winter they could see skiers flying through the air as they swooped off into nothingness. Boy, that was scary. She didn't know if she ever wanted to do that.

"Can I, uh . . . *may* I have a turn sitting by the window now?" she asked Gen.

"Sure thing," her sister replied. "I knew sooner or later you'd want to switch places with me. Any special reason?"

"I just like to be on the outside when we get to Lake Winnebago. It's fun to see the sailboats."

"Daddy," Ruthie said as she settled in by the window, "tell us about crossing the ocean when you came to

America." She loved hearing her dad recall his childhood. Every time she heard him talk about his early life she could almost see the hillsides and roads and the people he described.

"Weren't you scared to travel so far?" she asked for the hundreth time. She loved hearing his answer.

"Not really," Dad said. "Remember, I was 16 years old and ready for adventure!" He laughed almost as if he were laughing to himself. "You see, I was the older son in our family of four children there in the village of Misilmeri on the island of Sicily. And I spent my days working hard with my father in either his large garden or the lemon orchard."

"That's why you like lemons and lemonade so much, huh, Dad?" Ruthie asked. She just wanted to hear him say it again. She wanted to be part of his adventure.

Dad nodded and continued. "I wasn't afraid of hard work. That wasn't a problem for me. And we weren't starving by any means. But everyone kept hearing stories about America and how if you worked hard there, you could really get ahead! You could make lots of money. That appealed to all of us. From the time I was 6 years old I'd worked with my father as a street vendor. Even as a teenager I wondered, *Is this all there is to life?*"

"A street vendor?" Ruthie interrupted. "What's that? I forget."

"Well, our family sold our garden produce and our homemade wine in a stand at the side of the street. The others were content, but I was the boy with the wanderlust."

"What does *that* mean?" she asked.

"It means that I began begging and nagging and pleading with my father. I probably drove him to distraction."

"And if you keep asking questions, Ruthie, you'll drive Dad to distraction!" Steve laughed. "He won't finish his story until the middle of next year."

Ruthie made a face and poked him in the ribs. She didn't touch his face, though. She wouldn't do anything to hurt him or his scar.

Dad went on. "Finally, in 1902—when I was 16—Dad and I sailed for America. We were on a ship named the *City of Milan*. I was so excited. I still remember how I felt as I stood on the deck and waved goodbye to my native land."

Mom shook her head with compassion. "I feel for your mother and what she must have felt to say goodbye to you. Just think, having an ocean separating you from your husband and son!"

"Oh, yes. But I wasn't thinking about that. All I could think of was America."

"Did you sing 'O Solo Mio' when you were on the ship?" Ruthie couldn't seem to stop butting in. The story was so exciting to her.

Dad chuckled. "I may have. There was plenty of time to be whiled away. Fortunately for me, I was never seasick. So I spent many hours on deck watching the ocean, the people, and the sailors.

"When we approached New York harbor, you better believe that I was on deck to be sure that I saw the Statue of Liberty. What a beautiful sight that was. Some of the folk fell on their knees and thanked God for a safe voyage to a new land. Others cried with deep emotions, and all of us—every one of us—cheered loud and long. It was wonderful, and I will never forget it." The excitement in Dad's voice was obvious and unquestionable—he loved America!

"Where did you go when you got off the ship?" Steve asked.

"My father and I, and several other friends from our village, all lived in a big house at 246 Elizabeth Street. It was in what is now lower Manhattan.

"Most of us worked in the New York harbor, and we worked hard, I tell you. It was backbreaking. I was a hod carrier. That meant that I carried mortar and brick to the masons at their work sites. The bosses shouted out their orders, and we did our best to follow them. That's how we learned to speak English—swearwords and all. We learned and we earned! We could save a bit here and a bit there." Dad turned quickly to smile at his young daughter. "It was great! And as we became adjusted to our new surroundings we began to love the American way of life."

"Were there streetcars to ride?" Gen asked.

"Yes, once in a while we rode a streetcar. We lived pretty close to our work, so we usually walked. And I'll tell you, we treasured every cent we could get our hands on. But boys will be boys, and once in a great while we rode the trolley downtown just to see the sights of that big city. I had never seen Rome, Italy, but I was seeing New York," Dad laughed.

"Did you ever get lost?" It was Mom who asked this.

"Not that I recall," Dad replied. "Of course, we learned to read street signs and billboards. And there were signs on the outsides of the streetcars and signs on the insides. I remember that we were fascinated by store windows. You gotta realize that we fellas had come from a small town. All of the rush and busy traffic was exciting to us. Even the cop directing traffic with his whistle was dazzling to our country-boy eyes." He laughed again. "I never longed to be a cop, but I did like his uniform."

"New York must have been fun back then," Steve said, "but so was Chicago."

"True," agreed Mother. "After growing up in the small town of New London, I found living in Chicago very different. I must say I was intrigued by all the sights.

"I was determined that you and Genevieve would learn how to get around on public transportation. So I took you with me when I'd go down to the Loop, but I'd have you pretend you were taking *me*. I'd ask you to ring the buzzer when you saw that it was time to get off. You both learned so fast. I never worried about you after I was certain that you knew when to get off and get on."

"Mama, what's the Loop?" Ruthie questioned. "I forget."

"The Loop is the center of downtown Chicago," Gen answered immediately. "Oh, I loved Chicago."

"Of course, there were dangers, too," Mother reminded them.

"Like the time you gave me a nickel to buy a loaf of

bread at the corner bakery. Huh, Mom?" Steve exclaimed, a sparkle in his eye. "It seems funny to me now, but I sure was scared when it happened."

"Was that when you were robbed?" Ruthie asked.

"Yep, it was. A bunch of boys came up and started dancing around me like we were having fun. I was surprised and confused. Then one boy took one of my hands and one took the other, and of course, they found the nickel. Then off they went skipping and laughing, as if we'd just played a game!"

"Yeah, and Mom had watched it all happen from our living room window, never realizing that those boys were up to mischief until it was over," explained Gen. "It happened so fast that when she saw you running back toward the house unhurt she was relieved, weren't you, Mom?"

"It's true. Of course, I was disgusted about the whole escapade, but I truly was grateful those hoodlums didn't hurt you."

"I never saw those boys again," Steve said, "though I was on the lookout for them."

"Big cities are big cities all around the world," Dad joined in. "You learn all the tricks after a while. I think you and Genevieve are pretty much aware of your surroundings now. I don't worry when you ride the streetcars and buses. You've been trained always to know where you are and where you're going. To keep your eyes and ears wide open; to be always on the alert."

"I know how to ride the Number 12 streetcar clear downtown," said Ruthie proudly. "Mom and Aunt Bessie practiced with me. I even know how to transfer from one streetcar to another. I usually always ask the conductor for a transfer ticket, even if I know I probably won't have to use it. That way I have it if I need it."

"Yes," agreed Mom, "you get around just fine. And remember when my cousins Nellie and Irene came to Milwaukee to attend a teachers' conference? I sent you down to the train station to meet them all by yourself and bring them to our home on the streetcar. They were completely dumbfounded."

Ruthie giggled. "I remember."

"So, Dad," said Gen, "finish your story."

"Well, let's see. When after a year or so my father announced it was time we went home, I was not happy. Not happy at all! I didn't want to go back to Sicily and sell garden produce for the rest of my life. I told him that I wanted to stay in America, where I could find lots of other kinds of work.

"My father looked hard at me for a moment, but then smiled. He told me he couldn't go home and face my mother without me. But he said that he'd get me a round-trip ticket so that I could return to New York. That was agreeable to me." Dad was silent for a long moment. Ruthie wiggled, waiting for him for finish his story.

"And I have never had the opportunity to go back again," he said at last. There was another long pause. "Not on a minister's salary. My brother, Frank, writes to me now and again, but I haven't heard from him for quite some time. That's why I'm so worried about that dictator

Mussolini and the trouble he and Hitler are causing."

No one said anything for a moment. Each was lost in his own thoughts.

War! It was a dreaded word.

Dad's story and the family's conversation was so intriguing that Ruthie had lost all sense of time and was unaware of the scenery as they drove along. She even missed seeing Lake Winnebago and the Piggly Wiggly store in Oshkosh. She always waited to pass the store with the funny name.

"Weren't you glad to get home to Misilmeri, though, and see everybody when you went back with your dad?" Ruthie asked him. She could just imagine the hugging and the cheering, the tears and the laughter.

Dad nodded. "Certainly. It was wonderful. I stayed at home in Misilmeri for a couple of weeks. It was so good seeing my mother and brother and two sisters, but I was determined not to stay. I longed to return to America. I suppose that my uncles and aunts and cousins all thought I was a little crazy, but we did have a wonderful time while I was there.

"My little sister, Arcangela, was so sweet, and my brother, Frank, and I had the time of our lives. He asked all about America. That's when he decided that someday he'd come too."

"And he did, didn't he?" asked Ruthie, although she knew the story.

"He did indeed."

"But when Frank was here, times were very hard in America," Dad continued. "It was taking him a very long time to earn enough money for his wife and little girl to join him. And back in Sicily, they missed him. Here in America, he missed them. At last, he was so lonesome that he gave up and went home."

Everyone felt a little sad at that. It would have been fun to know Uncle Frank and their cousins. And only Dad could imagine what life had been like in Sicily in recent months. "I only hope and pray that my family is safe," Dad said a moment later. "These are desperate times, very dangerous times for those living in Europe right now." Dad's voice was filled with despair and distress.

Ruthie had seen pictures of Uncle Frank and his family. They had a little girl who was only a few months older than Ruthie herself. She was a bright-eyed, happy-looking girl, and Ruthie wished she could meet her and play with her.

Maybe she would be just as much fun as cousin Orrella, who was Aunt Bessie's granddaughter and lived in Chicago. (Bessie's daughter Helen was Orrella's mom.) Just yesterday Aunt Bessie had said that Helen and Orrella were coming for a visit later in the summer. That would be a happy day for Ruthie. Orrella was a live wire. At least, that's what Uncle Charlie called her—his live-wire granddaughter. 🌼

SEVEN

How Mom and Dad Met

Dad's voice brought Ruthie back with a start. "Something happened after I returned to New York that made me sit up in the middle of the night when I learned of it. I marvel at it yet."

Ruthie looked at Gen, and Gen nodded slightly and grinned. They both knew what to expect. Each time Dad told this story there were little different bits and pieces that they hadn't heard and that made the story exciting.

"It was two or three months after I came back to America that my mother wrote and remarked how happy she was that I was in New York. You see, not long after I left home my draft number came up. She was very glad that I was in America and not in the army! It was providential, children. The Lord definitely had a plan for me. He moves in mysterious ways."

All heard the reverence in their father's voice.

"Tell the children how you left New York and moved to Chicago," suggested Mom.

So Dad continued, much to the pleasure of the three in the back seat. They never tired of hearing his story.

"Two of my friends and I decided to move to Chicago, where we knew some people who'd come from Sicily. We had saved enough money for the journey and were sure that we could find jobs once we got there. So away we went! We were filled with vim, vigor, and vitality, I tell you.

"And we found work in the Gulbranson Piano Factory. I was put to work in the finishing department. I was trained how to use pumice stone to polish those beautiful pianos until they gleamed and shone like the sun. I gave that wood its last sheen. It was very satisfying work.

"We fellows were reliable, worked conscientiously, and didn't miss a day. A man from the Swedish Seventh-day Adventist Church worked in our department, and he befriended us. He saw that we were hard workers and must have liked that, for he gave us literature to read. Of course, by then we could speak and read English. To his delight, we all became Seventh-day Adventists. We actually had read ourselves into the truth."

Ruthie clapped her hands. Hooray for Dad!

"I was on fire for the Lord!" Dad continued. "As I shared this wonderful message with other friends, several of them decided that they wanted to be baptized. The upshot of it all was that some of the church leaders heard about me and wanted to know more." He laughed. "I guess they wondered who I was. Here I was, an immigrant kid who hadn't even been in the States very long. But I was so excited about the Lord and our special message that I couldn't help telling anyone who'd listen. Anyway, the church sent me to Broadview College for ministerial training. When I finished, my first assignment was to move to Milwaukee and pastor a small group of immigrants who were interested in keeping the Sabbath."

"Isn't that a beautiful story?" asked Mom. "I marvel at it every time I hear it."

The children all agreed.

"Now comes the part where you met Mama," laughed Gen, the girl with the romantic heart.

"That's right. Don't leave out the most important part of the story. Tell them how you met me." Mom put her hand on Dad's shoulder, then turned and looked toward the back seat. Her eyes sparkled with merriment.

"I'd better keep my eyes on the road," said Dad. "We're almost to the farm. Why don't you finish the story, Grace?" So Mom took up where Dad left off.

"It started with an announcement in the downtown Milwaukee church. A young minister was coming to town, and he would need help in his evangelistic series. Bessie and Charlie volunteered and attended the meetings from the very beginning. Charlie led out with the singing—you know he has a nice bass voice. Bessie played the piano. I was living with Bessie and Charlie at the time while I attended business college.

"To my surprise, one evening Bessie suggested that I take her place as pianist. She said that she didn't feel well. So I went with Charlie. I really think she planned that whole event."

Dad laughed. "Here, let me cut in!"

And before Mom could say another word, Dad continued. "You cannot imagine my surprise to see Charlie with this new young woman. He introduced her as his sister-in-law, Grace. And graceful she was! I was smitten with her from the start. Grace played the piano very well. She was pleasant, and well, I was immediately attracted to her."

"Pretty, too. Huh, Dad?" Steve teased.

"You're right there. I wanted to get better acquainted. I even rode home with her on the streetcar that night. It seemed like the polite thing to do, wouldn't you say? After that first night, Grace came to play for every meeting."

"She became your girlfriend, right?" Ruthie asked with a giggle.

"Yes, and then she became my wife."

"The rest is history," Mom happily told them.

"We're the history part, aren't we, Mama?" asked Ruthie, and the family all laughed.

"I have never regretted that back in Sicily I listened to that still small voice," Dad said seriously. "Living in America is a special privilege," Dad added. "I truly believe that God had a hand in the founding of this country and in bringing me here. As much as I love the land of my birth, this is now my home, and I'm happy to be an American citizen. Never take that privilege for granted, children."

Dad was always patriotic about his new homeland. He enjoyed every Fourth of July parade, and with his best tenor voice he would sing the national anthem with pride.

All of a sudden Dad jerked the car. "Oops, I almost passed the Larson Store corner!" He quickly turned onto the gravel road leading to the farm. Ruthie drew in her breath with a gasp. It had been a whole year since the families had visited each other. She could hardly wait!

Up ahead they saw the house and the big barn. Against the barn stood a tall silo with its shiny dome. The corncrib stood at the side of the barn. The chicken coop was partly hidden by the corner of the house. There was no sign of the cows because they were out to pasture, but Prince, the horse, was standing in the barnyard near the water tank.

Ruthie could hardly contain herself. "There's Carol! There's Ginny!" she called. "And here comes Dickie!" These were some of their cousins, Dell and Myrtle's children. Aunt Annie and Uncle Reynolds lived with their son Dell and his family.

Rover barked his welcome and bounded over to meet the car.

In no time at all Ruthie and Carol were holding hands and jumping up and down. Everybody was hugging everybody else. Aunt Annie and her daughter, Daisy, were hurrying from the house. Dell and Myrtle came running up, smiling and waving. And there was Uncle Reynolds with his battered straw hat scurrying around the end of the barn.

"Where's your bike, Carol? May I ride it?" Ruthie was so excited she could hardly stand still.

"It's in the shed with a flat tire," Carol said. "I rode it down to the Larson Store at the end of our road yesterday and must have ridden over a nail. Anyway, by the time I got home the back tire was flatter than a pancake. My dad can't fix it until he gets some stuff to patch the inner tube."

Ruthie looked dejected. "I was really hoping we could ride it. Oh well, let's go play in the hayloft," she said, and started running toward the barn. It was her favorite thing to do with her cousins.

"Wait, wait!" Carol cried, grabbing hold of Ruthie's hand. "I've got a surprise for you." Turning her young cousin around, Carol pointed to a swing set in the side yard.

"Your own swing set!" gasped Ruthie. She couldn't believe her eyes. At home she had to walk clear to her school's playground whenever she wanted to swing. All she had in her small yard was her tree. But of course she wouldn't want to give up that tree.

"Grandpa made the swing for us a few weeks ago out of some poles and rope. Come on!" So she and Ruthie ran to the swing, with Dickie tagging along.

Next to the swing set Grandpa had fashioned a small merry-go-round out of an old wagon wheel set atop a post. Dickie climbed right up on the wagon wheel and slowly turned himself around.

Gen and Ginny were so busy talking that they could hardly see where they were going. Steve and Dell carried the suitcases. Everyone was excited.

Steve was looking forward to work, even though he realized it would probably be his last summer at the farm.

As the women walked to the house, Ruthie overheard Aunt Annie telling Mom, "Now, Gracie, I have things all ready for you to bake apple pies for supper." Ever since she was a teenager Mom had been famous for her apple pies.

Grace's Apple Pie

About two hours ahead (or early in the day), prepare pastry for one 2-crust 9-inch pie.

To make the pie filling: Peel, core, and thinly slice about 2 pounds of apples (6 to 7 cups).

Then mix together:
- 1 tsp. cinnamon
- 1 cup sugar (use half brown sugar) or less (amount of sugar depends on tartness of apples)
- 2 tbsp. all-purpose flour

Place half the apples in the piecrust; sprinkle with half the sugar mixture. Top with rest of apples, then sprinkle with rest of sugar mixture. Dot with 1 tbsp. butter or margarine. Cover with top crust, sealing the edges and slicing vents for steam to escape.
Place in preheated 425° F oven. Bake 40 to 50 minutes until golden brown.

Serve warm or cold. Makes 6 servings.

"Welcome, Justus," Ruthie heard Uncle Reynolds say as he shook Dad's hand.

Dell patted Steve's shoulder. "We're glad to have you aboard, young man. We're going to need you this summer, especially when we cut the hay and load the wagon."

Steve burst out laughing. He'd told the family of his experience in loading the hay on his uncle's wagon during one of his first summers there. Because he'd often watched others doing it, he'd been really confident that he knew how to do the job, and thought that he didn't need any instruction. Before long, however, the entire stack of hay that he'd loaded fell off the wagon. Uncle Reynolds had to give him his first lesson in loading hay.

"And we've just acquired five new cows to add to the herd," Ruthie heard Dell say.

"We named one of those new cows Cherry," Dickie told Ruthie with a big grin, "because she has red spots!"

"Just as long as you don't call one of those cows Jenny, things will be OK," Ruthie laughed. "Gen doesn't want a cow with a name that sounds like hers."

"I had two rabbits last year," Dickie continued. He was eager to tell his cousin all the news. He was a cute little rascal with a round face and childish grin. "Bought 'em for 50 cents each. I thought I'd earn a little money."

"Wow, that sounds like fun."

"You would've liked them," he added. "They were cute and fluffy. I named them Peter and Polly Rabbit. Sure thought I could make some money raising and selling their baby bunnies."

"Where are they now? Ruthie asked.

"Well," Dickie said slowly, "those rabbits grew up real fast. I finally sold the whole lot of 'em—Peter, Polly, and all their 30 bunny babies. Only got a quarter for the whole bunch of 'em. It wasn't the best bargain I ever made."

He shrugged, and the girls sympathetically laughed with him.

EIGHT

A Day on the Farm

When they'd had enough swinging, the girls went to the barn and climbed up the ladder to the top floor, and then Carol checked the haymow for any rakes. When she was certain there were none stuck here and there in the hay, she and Ruthie climbed another ladder up the side of the granary to the very top. The top of the granary was wide and long and flat, so the girls could give themselves a running jump and land in the hay. They squealed and laughed until they could hardly catch a breath. Their cheeks were rosy red, and their hair was full of straw.

"You are the luckiest girl in the world to live on a farm," Ruthie told Carol. "What fun it is here!"

"It's fun, all right, but it takes a lot of work to keep it up." She plopped down in the hay. "That's why Grandpa and Dad are glad that Steve comes to help. They say that Steve's getting pretty good at all the chores."

Ruthie sank down beside her. "He loves coming," she said. "I just wish I could stay all summer too."

"Could you? Could you?" Carol squealed.

Ruthie looked sad. "No. Mama would never let me stay. She and Daddy would say I was too young."

The girls sat silently for a moment, both wishing they could be together all summer.

"Steve thinks it's fun to go to the New London church," Ruthie told her cousin. "We're related to lots of people there, aren't we?"

"Yeah, we sure are," Carol nodded. "My mom's told me that the old people at church were early members—a long time ago when it first started there. And their ancestors are our ancestors."

Ruthie looked puzzled. "My mom's told me about them too, but they're kind of hard to keep straight."

"I sort of memorized them," Carol said. "Our ancestors go back to Esek Eddy, who fought in the Revolution, and come down through the Turners and the Parfitts. James and Eliza Parfitt came from England, and we're descended from their son Henry and his wife, Marilla."

That fact Ruthie remembered. "Mama says that Gen's eyes are the same color as Grandma Marilla's," she said.

"Now the church is full of our cousins," Carol said, lying back in the hay. "I know them all."

"The old church building looks as if it were built right after the Flood," Ruthie told her, and they both laughed.

In the early afternoon Dad drove Aunt Annie and Mom to town to get a few groceries. Carol and Ruthie rode along just for fun. Aunt Annie got each girl a treat—a box of Cracker Jack. They chewed and talked at the same time, and before they knew it, all the Cracker Jack was gone.

On the way home Mom had Dad swing by Aunt Bessie Dexter's house. It was out of the way a bit, but neither Aunt

Annie nor Mom had seen their aunt for quite a while. She was a sister of their father, Henry, and the only one of the five children in the Parfitt family that was still living.

With hugs all around, Aunt Bessie warmly welcomed them into her quaint, small house. They visited only a short time, not wishing to be a bother, since they had not told her they were coming by. The thought came to Ruthie that she'd never seen anyone as old as Aunt Bessie, who was nearly 90. Ruthie had heard the family story about the daring girl who, quite by accident, had ridden a sturgeon clear across Parfitt's bayou and back! But that had happened 80 years before, when she was a little girl who'd just arrived from England. It was hard to see the laughing, adventuresome young Bessie in this elderly woman. Ruthie thought about that as they said goodbye and headed on back to the farm.

When it was time to bring the cows up from the pasture, Gen, Ginny, Carol, and Ruthie decided to do the job. Away they went, taking Rover with them. To Ruthie, walking down to the back pasture seemed as if she were walking into a picture postcard of rolling pastureland and meadows. It was so different from her neighborhood in the city.

As they walked Ginny said, "Know who's coming over for supper tonight while you're here? Lyle and Lulamae."

"They're cousins of ours somehow, aren't they?" asked Gen.

"Yeah, Lyle is the fellow who worked as a lineman and almost got himself killed."

"Seems as though I heard part of that story," Gen told her. "But what exactly happened?"

"Well, Lyle was up on a telephone pole, securely strapped by his safety belt. Somehow the pole got loose and began wobbling. He held on tight, and the pole fell with a whoosh! When the cross pole crashed into the ground, the force of the fall ripped Lyle right out of his belt. He hit the ground facefirst."

"Oh! Oh!" was all Ruthie and Gen could say.

"His face was smashed and his jaw was broken," Carol put in, "but the doctors fixed him up and wired his jaw, and he's OK. You'll see for yourself."

By now Gen was gripping Ruthie's hand tightly.

"The only thing you'll notice is that he uses a fork to eat. He never uses a spoon. His jaw was so broken that it was hard to put together. But the surgeon did his best, and you won't be able to see anything wrong just by looking at Lyle. He just can't open his mouth very far."

Ginny wagged her head. "It's a miracle he's still alive."

"I should say so," Gen agreed. "It'll be nice to meet him and talk to him."

Ruthie couldn't say a word. She was speechless.

As they neared the railroad tracks that ran across the back end of the farm, they found the cows grazing happily.

"Ca boss! Ca boss!" called Carol and Ginny.

Gradually the cows ambled toward them.

The cow named Cherry loved to go off by herself and

hide. When they discovered she was missing, Carol told Rover, "Go back and find Cherry."

He ran off. They waited, talking, just enjoying being out in the cooling afternoon. After a bit Rover returned with the vagabond cow, barking and fussing at her all the way. When any of the cows lingered or dawdled, Rover rounded them up, running behind them or nipping their heels. Then they'd plod forward, again heading for the barn. The cows knew it was milking time, so they didn't dillydally too long.

"Rover is the best dog I know," Ruthie said firmly.

"You heard what happened to our horse, Prince, didn't you?" Ginny asked them.

"I don't think so. Tell us," said Gen. She loved hearing animal tales as much as Ruthie did.

"Well," began Ginny, "when we finally got a tractor last year we didn't need for Prince to do the fieldwork anymore. Now he had time to roam the pasture and be free as a bird."

"Free as a bird!" Ruthie laughed. "That's funny."

"You're funny too," Ginny said, giving her a little poke. "Dad thought that it wasn't good for him be idle all the time, so he'd ride Prince down to the pasture, and they'd round up the cows. Then he'd give Prince a little workout doing odd jobs to give him some exercise. He didn't want him to get fat and lazy. That's not healthy," she added.

"After several days of this routine Dad went out one morning to get Prince so that they could bring the cows up from the pasture for milking. But to his surprise, he found all the cows standing there in the barnyard waiting for him. He just couldn't figure it out."

"The cows were all by themselves?" Gen's eyebrows went up in surprise.

"Yep," nodded Ginny. "This continued for several days, and it really puzzled Dad. So one morning he got up earlier than usual to find out what was going on." By now Ginny was laughing. "He caught Prince driving the cows up the lane. Once that silly horse got them into the barnyard, he turned and galloped back to the pasture."

The girls all had a good laugh at that one.

"Dad thinks he finally figured out what Prince was up to. If he brought the cows up to the barnyard all by himself, he wouldn't need to have Dad give him a workout. Dad says that animals are smart and can figure things out for themselves. They are more like people than we like to admit."

Ruthie and Gen were dumbstruck.

"Good old Prince!" Carol said proudly. "The horse that thought he was a dog."

"Now," said Ginny, "here's another good one for you. But this story's kind of scary."

"I don't care," said Ruthie, but she took hold of Carol's hand.

"OK. Carol and I were down here in the pasture rounding up the cows when the afternoon train came along." Ginny pointed back to the railroad tracks so they'd know just where it happened. "The engineer always waves to us, so we wave back."

"Do you know him?" Ruthie wondered.

"Not personally, but Dad says his name is Earl. Earl Slocum," Ginny explained.

"This time, though, the engineer waved differently," Carol said, joining in the storytelling. "He kept pointing back over his shoulder time and again. We looked, but didn't see anything strange down the tracks, so we just led the cows to the barn as usual."

"What on earth was he trying to signal?" Gen questioned.

"We found that out not long after we got home," Ginny went on. "After we got the cows to the barn, Carol and I went back to the house. About a half hour later, if that long, there was a knock at the back door. Grandma answered, and there stood a hobo."

"You're kidding!" exclaimed Gen. "Now, that's scary. We see beggars standing on a street corner once in a while, but we've never had one knock at our door . . . well, at least not since we've lived in Milwaukee."

"This guy was very bad off," Ginny said seriously. "He asked Grandma for some food. So she had him sit on the back stoop and gave him a big sandwich and a large glass of milk. He still seemed hungry, so she made him a second sandwich. When he asked if he could spend the night, Grandma told him to go to the barn and check with Grandpa."

"Dad thinks that Earl, the engineer, was warning us about the bum who was walking the tracks," Carol added. "Dad thinks that Earl didn't want us girls to be in any danger if the hobo was up to no good."

"Did he really stay all night? Did he say where he was going? What did he look like?" Ruthie and Gen were full of questions.

"Grandpa told him he could spend the night in the barn and sleep in the hay if he wanted to, and he did. Early next morning Grandpa went to check on him, but he was gone. We don't know when he left. His clothes didn't look too old or worn, but he hadn't shaved for several days. Dad said he figured the guy was a down-and-outer trying to find his way," Carol concluded.

"That's scary but sad. Maybe he was an angel and you entertained him unawares," Gen remarked thoughtfully, referring to the Bible text.

"I know that verse," Ruthie said. "It's Hebrews 13:2."

"Wow!" said Carol and Ginny together as they looked at their young cousin.

"Ruthie's learning all of the Sabbath school memory verses this year, and she'll recite them in church on the last Thirteenth Sabbath," Gen explained.

"Good for you!" said Ginny, and she patted Ruthie's back. "I wish I could be there to hear you, Ruthie."

"Me too," Carol chimed in. "I like Tony, and Mary, and Johnny, and all those kids in your church. They're fun."

Just then Rover added his bark-bark-woof-woof to the girls' voices. Cherry was lagging behind, so he loped after her.

"Boy, she's a dumb one," Carol laughed, "but Dad says she's a good milker, so we keep her."

"There was another bum that came by," said Ginny. "Remember him, Carol?"

"Oh, yeah. He was lots more scary than the first hobo. This fellow asked for food, and then wanted Dad to drive him into town."

"Yeah, he was a *real* tramp." Ginny's eyes sparkled as she continued the story. "Dad agreed to take him to town, so I slid into the back seat of the car and rode along."

"Ginny, you daredevil," Gen laughed.

Ginny giggled and nodded. "When we got to the outskirts of town Dad stopped and asked where he wanted to go. The guy asked to be taken to a tavern. At that, Dad told him that this was as far as he was going and to please get out. That fellow looked daggers at Dad and grumbled and squirmed around, but he finally got out of the car."

Carol excitedly interrupted, "Dad thought that the loafer acted as though he wanted to hit him, and that if Ginny hadn't been along he might have."

Gen and Ruthie couldn't believe their ears.

"I told Dad later that I was ready for that slouch," Ginny added. "I had the crowbar in my hand hidden under my sweater, and I would've used it on him if necessary." She laughed, but she added, "I'm not kidding. I did have the crowbar in my hand."

"Boy, oh boy, Ginny, you're the spunky one," Gen said in amazement as they started their walk back to the house.

That evening when Lyle and Lulamae arrived, Ruthie very casually looked at Lyle's face. Ginny was right. There was no trace of his injuries. And at the dinner table he acted like everyone else—eating with gusto but using only his fork. The conversation was lively and happy.

Amazing man! thought Ruthie. *I'd never believed it if I hadn't seen for myself.*

When it began to turn dark, Ruthie watched as Aunt Annie carefully lit each oil lamp. It was fun seeing her strike the match to light the wick and adjust the height of the wick for a brighter or dimmer light. This was something Ruthie had never seen at her house, where they had electric lights, but she thought that with her oil lamps in every room, Aunt Annie was richer than city folks.

Ruthie remembered that she'd heard Mom say that old things and old ways didn't need to seem strange to modern people. Yes, old ways might be different, but they weren't stupid or weird. You might even smile about old-fashioned ways of doing things, but you should never pity them. Rather it was smart to understand the way things were done in the past and the reasons for them.

For example, oil lamps were a nice improvement over candles, and people who'd had only candles to light their rooms would have been excited by the new oil lamps. Electricity had replaced the lamps, of course, and Mom had said that we could be thankful for that—and for other improvements that made our lives better. But she had also said that it was foolish to think that having modern things made you better or smarter than the people who'd lived before you.

Dad had smiled, and said that Mom was "philosophizing."

"Well," Mom had answered, "I guess it's just my way of putting into practice the old saying 'Be not the first by whom the new are tried, nor yet the last to lay the old aside.'"

In her young heart and mind Ruthie understood just what her mother meant.

Ruthie dreamed that night of oil lamps, tramps, and men with broken jaws. When she woke up in the middle of the night, she breathed a sigh of relief. She was in bed with Carol, so she closed her eyes and promptly went back to sleep.

Morning came too soon, for now they had to return home. Carol and Ruthie hugged and hugged again.

"Grace, do come when you can stay longer," Aunt Annie said as she hugged her youngest sister.

Everyone said thank you to everyone else. Last of all Ruthie gave Steve a special hug before she reluctantly climbed into the car. Her heart felt empty. She wished she could stay and play with Carol. And her big brother would be gone all summer. She already missed him, and they weren't even out of the yard.

NINE

One Spunky Girl

Not long after the trip to Aunt Annie's, some special visitors arrived at Aunt Bessie and Uncle Charlie's. Their daughter, Helen, came for a short visit from Chicago, and her own little girl, Orrella, came with her.

"We're gonna have so much fun," Orrella said. Orrella and Ruthie grabbed hands and jumped up and down as soon as Orrella got out of the car. Ruthie had been watching and waiting for her.

It wasn't going to be a long visit, but Ruthie and Orrella crammed as much activity as they could into just three days.

Orrella was just two weeks older than Ruthie, and the two of them played from early morning until it was finally dark. They jumped rope with Gloria and Mary Ann. They went to the school playground to swing and slide. Ruthie got out her newest set of paper dolls, and they played school with them. Best of all, they played jacks.

"Boy, Rella, you sure are good at playing jacks. You're just as good as Gloria, and that's good!" Ruthie exclaimed.

"Well, I play it a lot at home, that's probably why,"

Orrella told her. "I even play jacks on the top of my dad's desk. When he's not home, that is," she added with a grin. "But Grandma tells me that you're gonna learn 48 memory verses this year, texts and all. Forty-eight! That's a lot of verses. I don't think I could ever do that." She'd stopped bouncing the jacks ball as she talked. "Say some for me, OK?"

Ruthie wrinkled her nose. She didn't want to practice her memory verses right then. "There are so many other things we can do for fun while you're here," she protested. "Let's play the alphabet while we bounce my new tennis ball."

Orrella looked puzzled. "What do you mean, 'play the alphabet'?"

"Here, I'll show you. It's fun. Just wait a minute." Ruthie ran upstairs to her bedroom and got her new ball from the closet shelf. Then she ran back downstairs. "Come on outside," she called, "and I'll show you how to play it."

Ruthie bounced the tennis ball and said, "A. My name is Abbie, and my husband's name is Arnold, and we come from Alaska with a carload of apples." As she spoke, she swung her leg over the bouncing ball. Then she grabbed the ball and handed the ball to Orrella.

"You just say that sentence over and over, using the next letter in the alphabet. And each time you say any of the words with the new letter, you swing your leg over the ball, like this: 'My name is Abbie [swing], and my husband's name is Arnold [swing]'—just like that. You have to think of names and words that go with each letter of the alphabet. And if you struggle thinking of a name and hesitate at all, you lose your turn."

"I get it!" Orrella said, excited. "You have to think real quick and swing your leg at the same time. That'll be fun."

Ruthie nodded. "Yeah, it is fun. You take a turn now."

"OK, I'll try." Orrella gave the ball its first bounce. "B. My name is Bertha," she said, "and my husband's name is Bradley, and we come from Broadview with a carload of bananas." She looked at Ruthie, questioning. "Did I do it OK?"

"Oh, yes. Just keep going. You're on C. Go till you miss a swing or can't think of a word."

So Orrella continued. "C. My name is Connie, and my husband's name is Calvin, and we come from California with a carload of carrots."

"Good. Go on!" Ruthie urged. She loved this game.

"D. My name is Dorothy, and my husband's name is David, and we come from Denver, with a carload of dolls. E. My name is Ethel, and my husband's name is Evan, and we come from Elgin with a carload of eggs. F. My name is Phyllis, and my husband's name . . ."

Ruthie held up her hand. "Stop! Stop! Phyllis isn't spelled with an F. You're out. It's my turn."

Orrella stopped, but she was mad. "How do you know? Some girl may have spelled her name with an F."

"Do *you* know any girl that spells her name that way?"

"No, but it's possible."

"And I suppose you are going to say her husband's

name is Filip and they come from Filadelphia, right?" Ruthie all but stamped her foot. "Well, that's not the way we play it here."

"Let me keep going," Orrella said, and she started bouncing the ball. "G. My name is Gina and my husband's name is—"

"I quit," Ruthie fumed. "You're cheating. Give me my ball." Ruthie held out her hand, but Orrella just kept on bouncing, swinging her leg, and talking.

"You are so bossy," Ruthie cried. "I'm mad at you! You cheat!" She ran up the steps to the back door.

"I'm not a cheat! I'm just clever!" Orrella shouted, and she threw the ball on the ground.

Ruthie was so mad that she didn't even go after the ball. Without even looking back, she stomped up the stairs to the second floor and went to her bedroom.

Gen was in the kitchen stirring a big bowl of creamy rice pudding. "What's the matter, little sister?" she asked.

"Orrella doesn't play fair, and I'm mad."

"Well, cool off a minute. Go get a drink of water. Then think of another game to play. Learn to be diplomatic." Gen was good at thinking up different ways of getting along.

"What does *diplomatic* mean?" Ruthie asked. She didn't want to be it with Orrella, whatever it meant.

"It means that you learn to be positive and agreeable and get along with people. Why don't you get Orrella to play a different game and just forget about Phyllis with an F? You'll see. It'll work out." Gen couldn't help thinking that Orrella's misspelling of a girl's name was a little funny.

Ruthie brightened up immediately.

"Oh, Gen, you will make a wonderful teacher. I wish I could be in the school where you train children." Ruthie gave her sister a big hug. Admiration filled her soul. How lucky she was to have such a wise sister.

After finishing her drink of water, she ran back down the stairs. She picked up the ball and placed it on the stairway steps leading upstairs. Then she knocked on Aunt Bessie's door. Orrella answered immediately. She smiled.

"Let's go to the playground," Ruthie suggested. So after they got permission from their mothers, they ran off. Not a word was spoken about the recent tiff they had, but their fences were mended.

Gen's right. Sometimes it's best to move on. Ruthie's young heart soared. She was happy as a lark.

There were lots of things to do at the playground— monkey bars to climb, hopscotch outlines painted on the cement, ladders to climb, teeter-totters, swings. There were even two sandboxes.

Both girls headed for the swings. The swings were full, but they'd wait their turn. So standing well behind the yellow line painted around the swing sets, they waited. The line showed where it was safe to stand while waiting for the chance to swing.

Soon a girl jumped off and ran toward the merry-go-round. The girl next to her yelled, "Hey, wait for me," and jumped off of her swing too.

So Orrella and Ruthie jumped on and began pumping.

They laughed as they went higher and higher. After a while Orrella jumped off and ran over to the drinking fountain. Another kid grabbed her empty swing.

Just then a lanky boy came up to Ruthie. She had slowed her swing when her cousin jumped off, but Ruthie wasn't ready to stop yet. Now Olaf, the bully from Townsend Street, stood right in front of her. Ruthie recognized him immediately.

"Hey, you!" he said gruffly. "Get off! It's my turn."

"But I haven't been on very long," Ruthie protested. She kept swinging, pumping her legs so she'd go higher. "Anyway, it's not your turn."

Olaf grabbed the chain of her swing and took a step closer. "Well, get off anyway!"

All the kids nearby were watching as Ruthie reluctantly got off.

But before Olaf could even begin swinging, something happened. Orrella walked right up to where he sat in Ruthie's swing. Standing within inches of him, she glared up at his face.

"Who do you think you are, anyway?" she demanded fiercely. "Leave her alone. It's her turn. She waited in line. Why don't you do the same?"

The big boy's face twisted in a scowl. "Who says?"

"I say! Now get out of here."

Olaf glared back. "Do you know who you're talkin' to, skinny girl? I'm Olaf. Who are you?"

Orrella didn't budge an inch. Hands on her hips, she said calmly but strongly, "Now get this straight. I'm sayin' it only once. I'm Dr. Bowyer's granddaughter, and I'm from Chicago. Now I'm tellin' you—leave Ruthie alone. She's my cousin and she's stayin' on that swing, you good-for-nothin' bully."

Orrella grabbed the swing's chain right by Olaf's ear. She calmly stood there. She didn't move.

All the other kids stood amazed. Would Olaf retreat?

He hesitated, but then tossed his head, got up, turned on his heel, and walked off. He didn't look back.

The kids couldn't believe it. They gathered around the cousins and said, "Boy, Orrella, we wish you lived here all the time."

Ruthie cheerfully got back on the swing. *Now I'm glad that Orrella is stubborn and spunky*, she said to herself. And they had a wonderful time for the rest of the day.

The three days passed so quickly. Ruthie was sad to see Orrella leave to go back to Chicago. They hugged, and Orrella grinned. "'Bye, Rufie Biz-a-biz," she said. That was how she'd pronounced Ruthie's name when they were both small and she couldn't say Ruth Elizabeth.

Ruthie waved until their car was out of sight. "Come again real soon, Rella!" she called.

TEN

When Gen Cried "Help!"

In no time at all it seemed the summer was over. It was time to take Gen and Steve to Michigan.

"Two children in college at the same time; I can hardly believe it!" Aunt Bessie exclaimed as she hugged them both goodbye. "If you have time write once in a while."

Uncle Charlie hugged them too. "Your chin has healed well, Steve. Take care now. No one will ever notice it when you're up in the pulpit." He shot his nephew a teasing smile. He knew that Steve planned to be a preacher, just like his father.

"And Gen, be sure that everyone at college learns to speak the king's English!" Uncle Charlie laughed as he gave Gen's shoulders a hug.

Then they were off. It would be a long day's journey, but Ruthie looked forward to it. She especially liked riding along Lake Shore Drive in Chicago and seeing Buckingham Fountain. Gen and Steve knew the names of each of the tall downtown buildings. Ruthie liked the Wrigley Building just because she liked Wrigley's chewing gum. She grinned just thinking about it.

Lake Michigan was beautiful as always. She had grown

up being acquainted with Lake Michigan. It was one of the five Great Lakes of the United States, and was called that because it was so big. She thought it was fun that she could see Lake Michigan from Lake Park when she was in Milwaukee and from Grant Park when she was in Chicago. With the sun shining on the water's whitecaps, the view was spectacular.

As she rode along, Ruthie kept thinking about her own school year that was about to begin. Just daydreaming about it was exciting. There would be Doris, Dede, Neva Ann, Robby, Jerry, Jack, Allen, and, oh yes, Lyla. Ruthie felt thankful that Lyla was never in her room, but she was on the playground at recess. Oh, dread the thought!

When Dad pulled the car into Aunt Daisy's driveway, Ruthie was delighted. Aunt Daisy was another of Mom's older sisters. She and Uncle Gustave had four daughters. Rachel, the youngest, was a bit older than Gen. Gen had hopped out of the car, and she and Rachel were already hugging and talking a mile a minute. Aunt Daisy's older girls were already grown and gone.

"Do you have a swing for me, Uncle?" Ruthie asked as Uncle Gustave came from his work shed to greet them. He wiped his hands on a cloth and took her hand in his. She let him lead her to the backyard and into the shed. There she found a swing hanging from a rafter. It was just waiting for her. Uncle Gustave had hung it there, knowing that she was coming for a visit.

"Oh, thanks! Thanks so much!" She'd hoped for a swing, and knew there might be a swing. But to see it right there—she could hardly believe it. It would be so much fun to swing there in the shed. Without a word she grabbed the ropes and jumped on the swing. "Now I can watch you sharpen your tools while I swing," she sang out.

"You are very welcome, young lady. We're glad you are here!" He gave Ruthie a big smile, then turned to go back to the house to visit with everyone.

Uncle Gustave ran a sorghum mill next to the work shed, and Ruthie was fascinated with all his equipment. She wasn't allowed to play in the mill, but there were plenty of other things to do and places to have fun.

As she swung back and forth she recalled that the roof of this very shed was where Gen had almost lost her life. It had happened before Ruthie was born, but she'd heard it told many times.

Gen, Steve, and Rachel were playing outside. Someone had the idea that they should climb to the roof of the shed. Then they could open their arms and jump off. That would be a fun way to pretend to fly. Or so they thought.

But once on the roof, Gen stumbled. It was a small stumble, but to keep her balance she grabbed an electric wire strung along the window. Instantly she felt a buzzing shock and realized she couldn't let go. There was enough electric power in the wire that it held her fast.

"Help!" Gen had cried. "HELP!"

For an instant Rachel and Steve stood speechless, not knowing what to do. Then they both yelled, "HELP!"

Uncle Gustave and Aunt Daisy and Mother came running.

"Henrietta!" shouted Uncle. "Get me a rope from the mill!"

Henrietta was one of Rachel's sisters. She flew like the wind down the path to the mill.

Steve was scared and afraid for Gen. He knew she was in danger. He wanted to comfort her, so he reached out and touched her arm.

Uncle was climbing to the roof as quickly as he could. He saw Steve touch his sister. "Let Gen go!" he called. "Don't touch her!" He was afraid that the electricity would grab Steve and hold him fast, too.

At Uncle's command Steve dropped his arm.

Now on the roof Uncle scrambled to his feet, hurrying to get to Gen. Suddenly he realized that Steve had been able to let go. The electricity had not held him. So Uncle raised his arm and swiftly hit Gen's hand that held to the wire. Her hand dropped, and she fell into Uncle's arms. She was too weak to catch herself.

Carefully he climbed down the ladder and carried Gen into the house. He gently placed her on Rachel's bed.

"Are you OK, honey?" asked Mom. Gen nodded, her eyes wide with fright.

"I think so," she slowly whispered.

Everyone drew a breath of relief. She was going to be OK.

"Don't exert yourself until we see that your energy has returned," Mom told her, so that is exactly what Gen did. She lay quietly while the family tiptoed around her. It wasn't long until she felt like sitting up. Someone brought her a glass of water. Then she swung her legs over the side of the bed. She still didn't feel like playing, though. She had been too scared.

There was a small burn in the palm of her hand that had touched the live wire. And that hurt. Steve and Rachel plunked down on the bed next to Gen and began talking to her quietly, and the grown-ups relaxed for a bit in the living room, discussing the awful scare.

"Guess that wire didn't have as much power as the rest of the wires on the house have," Uncle observed.

"It's a miracle that we still have her with us," Dad said, his eyes shining with tears.

Gen's hand healed in time. In the end, all she had to show for her frightening experience was a tiny scar in the middle of her palm.

Ruthie stopped swinging when she heard her mother calling for her to come to the car. She said they were going to the campus to get Steve and Gen moved into their dormitories. Then they'd go to a nearby orchard and buy a couple bushels of Red Haven peaches to take home and can so they'd have fruit to eat during the winter. ❁

ELEVEN

A Friend Named Esther

 School was starting, and Ruthie was glad. As much as she enjoyed summer vacation she was always ready for school to start in the fall.

"I can't believe summer is over," Mom said on the first day of school. "But the lovely golden maple leaves say that fall and winter are on their way."

Ruthie darted out the door and met Mary Ann, who was waiting for her. "I'm so glad to be going to school again. Are you?" Ruthie asked.

Mary Ann nodded her head. "I agree. I love school too."

As they walked along they began to sing the ABC song that they had learned from one of the children's radio programs they listened to.

Always be careful; that's the meaning of the ABCs.
Always be fearful when you're not in Mother's company.
We know you kids must have your fun, but please don't ever run
Out in the street where automobiles you see . . . Remember
Always be careful; that's the meaning of the ABCs.

95

Old Clyde Marshall, one of the school's janitors, heard them coming along. He had been sweeping away the freshly mowed grass from the sidewalk. He stepped aside and smiled his funny smile—his whiskers spreading and his bushy eyebrows raised high.

"Mornin', young ladies," he greeted them. "Nice to hear ya singin' so brightly. Hope you have a good day."

The girls smiled and nodded politely as they skipped along. When they were out of earshot, Mary Ann said, "I wonder why he doesn't shave. He doesn't have a big, long beard, but it's clear as day that he doesn't intend to get rid of what he has."

"Do you think he knows that it makes him look old?" Ruthie wondered.

"Probably. But he must not care. He's nice, though," Mary Ann added thoughtfully.

As they neared the school Ruthie could see Neva Ann, Dede, and Doris coming from the other direction, so they waved to one another. Mary Ann's classroom was at the opposite end of the building, so she entered the school by another door. She said, "So long!" and ran off so she'd be on time.

As Ruthie and her classmates stood and talked together, Lyla Aldrich ran up and joined them.

Wonder what she wants, Ruthie thought. *No one asked her to join us. Why doesn't she go talk to the girls in her class-room? They're standing right over there.*

Lyla wasn't in Ruthie's circle of friends, but didn't seem to understand that they felt she was an outsider.

Even if she had, it would have made no difference. She came across as snobbish and bossy. In fact, Ruthie thought Lyla liked making them uncomfortable. *I wonder why she even lowers herself to talk to us. Maybe because the other girls in her room don't take the time to be around her,* Ruthie mentally pondered. *Wish she'd just leave us alone. I know, I know, I should be more gracious.* So Ruthie looked at Lyla and smiled.

Just then the bell sounded, and everyone quickly got in line. Pearly ran up and jumped in just ahead of Robby. She turned and gave him an empty grin. He politely nodded, but didn't say a word.

"Oh, there's Pearly," said Ruthie to herself. "I almost forgot her. At least she's not a bother like Lyla. Not in the same way, anyhow." Pearly had a hard time learning and a hard time listening.

The kids went into the school, stopping their jabbering and quietly forming a single-file line. This was their routine. They did it every school day. In single file they climbed the wooden stairs to the second floor and went to Mrs. Armstrong's cloakroom. There they hung up their sweaters and proceeded into the classroom.

Mrs. Armstrong had a big smile for each of them, and school began for the day. Ruthie was glad to be sitting in front of Robby and just behind Neva Ann. The three were good students and enjoyed rivaling one another.

Neva Ann was a bright girl too. Her folks owned a neighborhood bakery, and Ruthie loved the way her friend smelled sweet and sugary. Her dresses were always neat as a pin, and she wore a bow in her hair every day—not just a barrette. Lyla always looked Neva Ann over to see what she was wearing. It made Neva Ann a bit self-conscious, but it made Ruthie annoyed. Who did Lyla think she was, anyway? Some fashion expert? But no angry words had ever been exchanged, at least not yet.

Dede sat across the aisle on one side of Ruthie, and Doris sat on the other side.

I just love being surrounded by my best friends, Ruthie thought. *This will be a spectacular year, I just know it.*

After they repeated the Pledge of Allegiance, spelling class began. The day progressed as usual. Mrs. Armstrong was an excellent teacher. She just would not tolerate misbehavior. Even Bernie knew better than to get on the wrong side of Mrs. Armstrong. Bernie was one of the better-behaved Townsend Street boys. He could be a good student whenever he tried, but he loved fun and mischief.

There were two new girls this year, Esther and Patti. They sat by the windows. Patti was a cute girl, small for her age, with short, blond hair. She was nimble, lively, and quick. She had a perky way about her that the kids took to immediately.

Esther had brown curly hair and serious brown eyes. As the days passed, the kids saw that she was a little shy. She never went out of her way to be friendly, although she did not look disagreeable. She paid attention to what the teacher said, but Ruthie couldn't tell if she was a good student or not. She kept her eyes on her book or her work. She rarely talked with anyone.

Ruthie was puzzled. If someone spoke to Esther, she always answered. She was polite, and sometimes she'd smile. But she never started a conversation.

"Oh, well, not everyone's like Patti, I suppose, for it takes time to get used to a new school and new kids," Ruthie said to herself.

At recess Ruthie and her friends played the usual game—boys chase the girls. Everyone ran around, kind of like a game of tag. If a boy caught a girl, she had to go to jail and sit on a certain cement basement window ledge. Then when all the girls got caught, the game reversed, and it was girls chase the boys. But that game hardly ever got far, because recess would end.

The game was fun. Dede could always sneak out of jail! Finally the boys appointed Jerry as a full-time jailer to guard her when she got caught. But that didn't always work. Dede could sneak out of jail better than anyone else. All of a sudden they'd see her running around again—free as a bird and just as happy.

On the second day of school Neva Ann had brought a jump rope. She and Ruthie had always been the rope-jumping champions. But then at recess Patti pulled out a jump rope of her own and began doing some fancy steps. She was amazing. Agile little girl that she was, Patti could jump like a circus expert.

"Wow, Patti, you're good. Show us how you do it," the girls begged.

"Let's jump double Dutch with two ropes," Patti suggested. "Here, Ruthie, take my rope. Neva Ann, we'll use your rope, too. You and Ruthie begin turning both ropes like an eggbeater, and I'll show you."

So the lesson started. Cleverly Patti jumped in double time, turning circles and occasionally rhythmically touching the ground in between her jumps. Or she'd swing a foot up and slap the sole of her shoe while jumping with only one foot. Yet she never missed a beat.

The girls shouted, cheered, and clapped. Even some of the boys came to watch.

Esther stood nearby.

"Come on, Esther!" Ruthie called. "Come join us." Esther hesitated at first, but then joined in.

For the next several days Ruthie, Neva Ann, Doris, Dede, Patti, and sometimes Esther all jumped to their hearts' content. They made quite a team. Before long they could put on a playground extravaganza. Robby and his buddy Jerry called them the Jumping Jacquelines.

Then one day during afternoon recess Ruthie saw Esther sitting alone on a basement window ledge. Afternoon recess was not long enough to get into a game, but Ruthie never was one to sit still. "Esther, let's play on the monkey bars," Ruthie called. Esther jumped up and followed. As they walked Esther said in her quiet way, "You are so nice to me, Ruthie. I like you."

"Well, thanks; I like you, too."

As the days passed, Ruthie and Esther often talked. Esther was not usually interested in running and playing, as Ruthie was, but she turned out to be quite a conversationalist whenever they happened to be alone together.

"I have a suggestion, Ruthie," Esther announced one day. They were alone, playing a quick game of hopscotch. "How about you pretending you are half Jewish, and I'll pretend I'm half Gentile. Wouldn't that be nice?"

Ruthie was puzzled. What a funny thing to say. "Why?" she asked. "It wouldn't change our friendship any."

Esther looked down at the ground. "It's just that I wouldn't feel so lonesome if I pretended to be half Gentile and you pretended to be half Jewish. We'd be the same."

Ruthie slowly nodded. She hadn't thought much about it, but Esther was Jewish. And Ruthie had heard about the trouble Jews were having in Germany and other places in Europe. A lot of people didn't like Jews.

"You are one of the friendliest kids to me," Esther went on. "My heart feels special toward you."

"Well, how about that!" Ruthie laughed. "My heart likes you, too. Is there any more to this pretend game?"

"No, but whenever I look at you from now on, I will feel good all over," Esther said. Her eyes sparkled.

"We do both have Bible names. I hadn't thought of that before," Ruthie said thoughtfully. "And I keep the Sabbath, just as you do. I'm a Seventh-day Adventist."

Esther was serious. "I never heard of that church before, but it must be a nice one if the people are all like you." She gave Ruthie a wide smile. "From now on, things will be special between us. OK?"

"OK!"

The bell rang, and the girls ran to get in line at the school door.

TWELVE

A Nosy Girl

 It was Tuesday. And after recess on Tuesdays Ruthie had orchestra practice. Several other kids played instruments too, so they'd all march down to the band room, where Mr. Germain, the conductor, waited for them.

Doris was a fine little musician. It was her influence that made Ruthie want to take violin lessons. Doris had first chair in the first violin section. That meant she was the best. She played the piano, too. Ruthie thought she played piano almost as well as Gen did. Doris's father taught piano and violin, and everyone could see that Doris was talented.

Ruthie had been taking violin lessons for only a year. On Thursday afternoons she and Allen left school early. They'd catch the streetcar and ride to the Clarke Street School for their violin lessons.

In the school orchestra Ruthie and Allen sat in the second violin section. Ruthie longed for the day when she could play well enough to be with Doris.

All the orchestra students could see that Mr. Germain loved music. He'd tell them about the different composers and hum the melody of the new pieces they were learning to play. And he was not afraid to tap his baton on the music stand when they didn't play correctly or weren't paying close attention.

"Let's do that over again," he'd say, "and think of soldiers marching when you play. This is not a waltz or a dance. This is a military song. So play lively and keep strict time!" Somehow he made the music come alive by explaining the theme of the music and how the composer came to write a particular piece.

Even though he made them work hard, the kids liked him. He could be funny and joke with them, and he praised them if they did well. The whole school looked up to the members of the orchestra. It was something important to be good enough to play with the orchestra. And once or twice a semester they'd put on a short concert for the entire school.

Yes, music was special to Ruthie.

"Mom, Lyla Aldrich is so nosy," Ruthie said to her mother one day after school. "She annoys me."

"Who's Lyla? I don't recognize her name. I don't think you've mentioned her before." Mom was puzzled.

"Well, Lyla's not in my class. She's in Mr. Siewert's room, but we have recess together, so I see her every day. She's nosy."

"How's that? In what way?"

"Well, today she asked Neva Ann how much she paid for her new scarf. Now, isn't that nosy?"

"True," Mom replied. "It really is none of Lyla's business. Did Neva Ann give an answer?"

"She didn't answer at first, and I could tell she wasn't happy, but Lyla is such a snob. She's like a persecuting attorney. She asks way too many questions. None of us like her very much."

Mom chuckled. "I think the word you're after is *prosecuting* attorney, Ruthie, not persecuting. There is a difference."

Ruthie grinned, just thinking about her mistake. "Well, Lyla is a pest. She thinks she's so smart. She does have better clothes than the rest of us, but that doesn't make her better than we are. We girls all agree about that!" Ruthie was so disgusted she almost stomped her foot. "Sometimes she asks me impertant questions, too. She knows I don't like it, but she just asks anyway."

Mom couldn't help laughing out loud.

"Oh, Ruthie! You can be so funny. Your sister Genevieve surely influences you and helps broaden your vocabulary."

Gen was a great reader. For Gen, learning was fun.

Ruthie's face broke out in a broad smile. "What did I say wrong this time?"

"The word is *impertinent*, not impertant. And, yes, I will agree," Mom told her. "Asking personal questions is impertinent and out of line. It is not socially acceptable behavior. Here's what to do. Next time Lyla asks you about the price of anything personal, especially clothes, just turn your eyes away from hers and continue talking to the other girls. Act as if you haven't heard her."

Ruthie thought for a moment. "But what if she asks me again, demanding-like? Then what should I do?"

"Ignore her. You don't have to look daggers at her, just don't answer. No matter how many times she asks, do not answer. If you are alone with her, say, 'Excuse me,' and walk away. She'll catch on that she cannot persuade you to answer her."

Mom reached out and drew Ruthie close. "It's one thing if you and a close friend are talking. Maybe she's telling you about a bargain. But it's quite another if someone demands to know what you paid.

"I knew a girl in our Chicago church who would not acknowledge a prying question, no matter how brash the girl who asked it was. I remember that several girls were chatting when this one girl brazenly asked Mary the cost of her dress. Mary acted as though she didn't hear the question."

"Was the girl poor?" Ruthie put in.

"Oh, no. The inquisitive girl wore very nice clothes. In fact, her father earned more than any of the other fathers. She asked three times, and three times Mary ignored the question. Finally the rude girl caught on that she was getting nowhere. I'm telling you, honey, it works."

"I can do that too," Ruthie said. "I'll be prepared for Lyla next time. She's meddling into other people's business, isn't she?"

"Absolutely!" Mom answered. "Show tact and diplomacy, but never allow yourself to be pressured by anyone who is going beyond the bounds of decency."

THIRTEEN

Music in Her Head

 The school days followed one after another. September turned into October. November was right around the corner. And just then the teacher changed the classroom seating arrangement. All of a sudden every student sat in a different place. And Mrs. Armstrong had placed Pearly right behind Ruthie.

Ruthie stood it until recess. Poor Pearly had a hard time learning and a hard time listening. She loved to whisper and giggle. Ruthie couldn't keep her mind on her own work. So when the kids went out to recess, she lingered at Mrs. Armstrong's desk.

"Mrs. Armstrong," began Ruthie. She was hesitant, but determined to say what was on her mind. "Why do I have to sit next to Pearly? She is such a nuisance."

Ruthie felt sorry for Pearly, but felt so annoyed.

"Please change my seat, Mrs. Armstrong," Ruthie pleaded. "She's a pest."

"That she is, my dear," agreed Mrs. Armstrong, "and that is why—for the time being—I have seated her behind you. I'm wanting her to have a good example."

In Ruthie's eyes, that was not a good reason.

"Do I have to sit by her all the rest of the semester?" she asked with wide eyes.

"Probably not. But you understand that Pearly has special learning needs. She must have someone show her how to behave."

Ruthie nodded.

"I'm asking you a favor. Are you willing to help me?" Mrs. Armstrong squeezed Ruthie's hand.

"All right. I'll try," Ruthie replied soberly.

"That's my girl. I knew I could count on you."

"But I don't think it will work. Pearly is so stubborn."

"Yes, she is. I'll tell you what to do. Don't answer her or act as if you know she is there behind you. Just keep your eyes on your work or on me." The teacher smiled kindly, and Ruthie politely nodded.

"By the way, Ruthie, while we're together, I have something to propose to you. During our school's annual Christmas program I wonder if you would direct a small choral group of your classmates while they sing a song. How does that sound to you? I will select the singers, and I'd like for you to direct. How about it?"

It didn't take Ruthie long to agree. At first she asked, "In front of the entire school, and in front of all the parents?" But then she nodded quickly. "I've never done it before, but I'd love to try." Anything musical appealed to Ruthie. The fear she felt at first was short-lived.

"That's a good girl. I'll begin working on this. In the meantime, don't worry too much about Pearly. Just do your best to concentrate."

"I'll try, Mrs. Armstrong. Guess she's my cross to bear," Ruthie said soberly.

Mrs. Armstrong could not help smiling.

❧

Ruthie couldn't stay sad long. After school she ran home to tell about the directing assignment. "Imagine! Me, a music conductor!" she said with a proud grin.

"It won't be the first time you conducted music, Ruthie," Dad chuckled. Ruthie somehow knew he was joking.

"What? When did I ever conduct?"

"You directed the symphony in Chicago during the World's Fair when you were only about a year and a half old," he told her.

"Aunt Daisy and Uncle Gustave were with us. We were sitting way up in the stands. You sat on my lap so you could see. At first you just listened and bobbed your head, but then you began to swing your little hand in perfect time. They were playing one of John Philip Sousa's famous marches. Everyone around us smiled as they watched you," Dad added. His eyes gleamed with pride as he spoke.

"We were all quite proud of you, Ruthie," Mom put in. "You've had music in that head and heart of yours ever since you were a baby." Mom lightly pinched Ruthie's cheek. "You even hummed to yourself in your crib."

"I hummed when I was a baby?" Ruthie was surprised. "Really, Mom?"

"You surely did. One afternoon Gen quietly came running to me and asked me to come to the bedroom door-way. Then she stopped me and put her finger to her lips. I stood and listened to you hum as you were drifting off to sleep. Now, that's the truth, Ruthie. You amazed us all."

Ruthie couldn't help smiling with satisfaction. She'd hummed when she was a baby. She surely hadn't known *that*.

What Ruthie *did* know was that she really loved music. Whether a choir, an orchestra, or bands playing a lively march, Ruthie loved it all.

At recess the next day Ruthie confided in Doris. "Mrs. Armstrong asked me to direct a music selection during the Christmas program this year. Can you believe it?"

"Of course I can. You're a good musician. Even my dad says so."

Doris knew from experience. Sometimes she and Ruthie walked home from school together, and they'd play their violins together just for fun. And once they'd played a duet during a school program—Beethoven's "Minuet in G." The kids had clapped loud and long when the girls took a bow together.

"Mrs. Armstrong couldn't have picked anyone better than you, Ruthie."

"Except you, Doris." Ruthie smiled sincerely.

"Well, Mrs. Armstrong asked me to be the group's lead soprano. I'll keep my eyes on you and never miss a beat."

The girls linked arms and walked around the playground.

"That new girl, Esther, is very nice but quiet. Let's go talk to her," Ruthie suggested, but just then Lyla hurried up to them.

"Just what are you two bosom buddies up to now?" Lyla asked. Ruthie was not charmed by Lyla's attention or her crude speech. The word *bosom* was not in the children's vocabulary. It was considered improper.

"We're just talking," Doris replied.

Just then a boy running backwards to catch a basketball slammed right into Lyla, and they both fell down.

Lyla jumped up. "You clumsy idiot!" she yelled. "Why don't you watch where you're going?"

It was a boy from sixth grade, tall for his age. "I'm sorry," he said breathlessly as he ran off, throwing the ball to a teammate.

Lyla trudged over to the bubbler and rinsed off her scratched arm. It wasn't a big scratch, but she was unhappy, and Ruthie could understand why. She watched her for a moment, then turned to Doris. "There's still a few minutes of recess left. Let's go see what Esther is doing."

❦

One day after orchestra practice Mr. Germain called Ruthie aside. Except for Doris, who was waiting for her friend, the room was empty of children.

"Ruthie," the music teacher said, "Mrs. Armstrong has asked me to give you some pointers about conducting."

"Oh, Mr. Germain," implored Doris quietly, "may I stay and watch?"

"I don't mind if Ruthie doesn't. How about it, Ruthie?"

"I'd like to have her here for encouragement" was Ruthie's wide-eyed response.

"Fine. Doris, you sit in the back of the room. Now, I don't want to hear a squeak out of you," he added with a smile. Mr. Germain was a good-natured man, and the children admired him.

First he showed Ruthie how to hold the baton and how to count and beat the time. "Three-quarter time and four-four time are the most common," he explained.

"Here, give it a try," he said, handing her his baton. "You direct, and I'll sing." He winked at her. Ruthie smiled and rolled her eyes.

"Don't be bashful, Ruthie," he told her. "I know your ability. You'll do fine. Let's do 'The First Noel.' That's familiar to you. You don't even need to look at the music.

"OK," he said. "Up with the baton. This is three-quarter time, so your arm will draw a triangle in the air, just as I showed you. Hold the baton up and pause to get my attention. Then when you begin, I'll start singing."

Ruthie did as he said, and was pleasantly surprised. Directing wasn't that hard to do.

"Good girl! You have a great sense of rhythm." Mr. Germain's praise was music to her ears. The teacher had her practice directing other Christmas songs, too. When she left the orchestra room, she felt as if she were walking on air.

"You caught on quickly," Doris told her as they walked down the hall. She was always lavish with her praise. "I don't even care if Mrs. Armstrong scolds me for not coming right back to class after orchestra. I'll tell her Mr. Germain needed me to give him some pointers."

The girls laughed and linked arms. Then they stopped at the bubbler and drank some cold water before returning to their classroom.

❦

As the days turned into weeks, Ruthie noticed that Mrs. Armstrong spoke more often to Pearly. Sometimes she would walk down the aisle and stand near Pearly's desk. And little by little, Pearly began to quiet down. After a while Ruthie almost forgot that Pearly sat behind her. Finally came the day that the teacher moved Pearly to a different desk.

As Ruthie left the room to go home that afternoon, Mrs. Armstrong smiled at her and mouthed the words "Thank you!"

FOURTEEN

Newsboys on Hopkins Street

 One day an announcement was made on the radio that Gimbel's Department Store was going to have a three-day Christmas show. Gimbel's was a very large store, and well known for their beautiful holiday decorations. They were bringing in two elephants to perform for their customers. A prize was promised to the child who suggested the best names for the elephants.

All the schoolkids were excited. After the announcement no one seemed to talk of anything else.

"Are you going?" was the question most asked. And all the kids planned to go.

"An elephant show!" Robby had exclaimed. "Just tell me how Gimbel's plans to get two elephants up to the third floor!"

That wasn't something that Ruthie or too many of the other kids worried about. But they were interested in the Name the Elephants contest. None of them had decided to submit names, however. They were just interested in hearing about it.

"Will you enter the naming contest, Robby?" they asked.

"Sure," he quickly replied. "I'd name one Tree and the

other one Trunk. That ought to get the grand prize."

"That Robby! His brain must run 50 miles an hour," Ruthie whispered to Esther. From then on they all referred to the Gimbel's extravaganza as the Tree-Trunk Show.

Before Thanksgiving Aunt Bessie and Mom began sewing a new dress for Ruthie to wear at the school Christmas program. Mom and Aunt Bessie had gone downtown to the Boston Store and together selected a pretty wool plaid of maroon and dark green. A white thread highlighted the darker colors. They took special care to lay the pattern so that all plaid lines met exactly at the seams. Their older sister Daisy had taught them to sew.

To make sure that the dress fit just right, Ruthie had to try on the dress time and time again. That wasn't fun. It seemed that every day she had to have another fitting. Standing on a chair so that Mom could mark the hem was the final struggle. She tried hard to stand straight and not wiggle, but it was boring.

Then one day when she came home from school Ruthie found the new dress hanging in her bedroom. She walked up and let her hand drift over the skirt. It was beautiful. Then her mouth opened in surprise. Mom had crocheted a "loverly" white lace collar. Ruthie was flabbergasted. The dress looked just like a picture in the mailorder catalog. It was ready well before the program, so she had a long time to enjoy looking at it before she'd wear it.

Aunt Bessie came upstairs, and Ruthie put on her new dress and paraded around the kitchen while Mom smiled her approval.

"You look lovely," Aunt Bessie said. "But remember to be just as nice on the inside as you look on the outside. As my father used to say: 'Pretty is as pretty does.'"

Ruthie nodded. "I know." She looked at her mother. "Mom says the same thing too."

One evening just before supper Ruthie plopped herself on the floor in front of the old radio in the dining room. She leaned against its dark wooden cabinet and placed the book she'd been reading on the floor between the tall spindle legs. She thought the legs were elegant looking, the way they were carved.

But Mary Ann's father had just bought a new radio that was really sleek looking. It was a bit taller and wider, and the cabinet had no spindle legs—it was solid all the way to the floor. But it was a Zenith radio. Both their fathers thought that Zenith was the best radio to be had. So did Uncle Charlie.

However, Dad had said if he ever replaced their old radio, he would get a small Zenith tabletop radio. He had seen one at the department store downtown, and he had told Mother it would fit just fine on the slim end table that Mother had purchased in a Goodwill store when she and Aunt Bessie had gone shopping there. The end table had spindle legs, too, and a nice smooth top that Mother had covered with one of her crocheted doilies. Mother and Dad had agreed that the end table with the radio on it would look nice when tucked in next to the overstuffed armchair in the living room. And it wouldn't take up as much room as the big old radio.

Ruthie read another page in *Little Women*, then let her mind go back to the furniture. Ruthie thought it was fun to listen to the grown-ups talk about arranging a room. Mom and Aunt Bessie would sometimes sit and discuss how this piece of furniture or that piece of carpet would really enhance or improve the look of a certain room. Not that they had the money just now to be buying carpet or furniture, but they could picture things in "their mind's eye," as they often said.

Sometimes they'd rearrange their furniture and then ask the other how she thought it looked. Would this chair be better in a corner or next to a certain table? Gen would look at Ruthie with a twinkle in her eye when the two "Parfitt" sisters discussed how this or that change would be more refined or better suited to their idea of good taste.

Ruthie hoped the new radio—if and when they ever got it—would have better reception. The old radio had static now and then, and Dad said it was wearing out. But it was the only radio the family had ever had, and Ruthie knew she would miss it. She liked the design of the heavy fabric that lined the nicely carved front underneath the dial. So almost unconsciously she closed her book and stroked a spindle leg as another exciting adventure of *Jack Armstrong, the All-American Boy* came on the radio. It was her favorite program. She especially liked to hear the music that played after each daily episode—the ABC song that she and Mary Ann enjoyed.

Just as the program ended, Dad came into the room. "I need for you to move over," he told her. "I want to listen to the radio. The news is coming on, and I want to hear what's going on in Europe."

Ruthie stood up and stretched. "OK," she said. But it wasn't really OK to her. "I wanted to listen to *The Lone Ranger* next," she muttered quietly as she crossed the room. But she knew better than to protest too loudly.

These days Dad always wanted to check on what was happening over in Germany. That dictator Hitler was still stirring up trouble. *Bad trouble*, Dad and Uncle Charlie called it, and they followed the news with great concern. In fact, day after day they tried to analyze the newspaper stories and what the radio commentators said about the trouble in Europe.

Ruthie watched Dad twirl the big dial until he came to his favorite news station. Then he sat down and leaned forward so he could hear every word. Sometimes the voices from overseas would echo and sound scratchy, so Dad would put his ear near the speaker. Sure enough, here came the voice of the newsman Dad always listened to. Ruthie sighed and went to the kitchen, where Mom was preparing supper.

"Is it really that bad? This war in Germany?" Ruthie asked.

Now it was Mother's turn to sigh. "Yes, indeed it is," she said. "I'm so glad that the United States is not yet involved. Poor England is suffering through some serious turmoil."

Ruthie picked up a piece of carrot and popped it into

her mouth. "What do you mean—turmoil?"

"Oh, my child, Germany is bombing London. Air-raid sirens go off really loud so people know to hurry to bomb shelters. This is a war." She paused, took a deep breath, and repeated quietly, "This is a war."

It was after supper that they heard Uncle Charlie's quick footsteps, then a loud rap at the door. "Justus! Justus!" he called. "Turn on your radio."

Dad reached the door in two strides and jerked it open. "What is it?" he asked, fear on his face.

"The Japanese have bombed Pearl Harbor, and President Roosevelt is speaking right now."

Dad snapped on the radio. Together he and Uncle Charlie hovered close to its speakers, listening to the U.S. president's dreadfully serious voice. Ruthie sank into a chair, her eyes on the two men. She didn't understand what was happening.

Her mother's moan pulled her attention away from the radio voice. "Oh, this is awful," she cried, and there were tears in her eyes. "Our country has been attacked!"

Ruthie shook her head. She knew her geography. "Hawaii is very far away, Mom. It's not near us. It's not even one of the 48 states."

By now Mom was standing next to Dad in front of the radio. "Hawaii belongs to the United States," she said in a whisper, "so it's just the same as attacking us." Then she turned her attention back to the radio.

Later that evening something strange began happening in their neighborhood. Newsboys walked their quiet street shouting, "Extra! Extra! Read all about it! Pearl Harbor bombed!"

Never in Ruthie's memory had the newsboys sold papers up and down Hopkins Street. They did all their shouting on downtown street corners near their newsstands. Something was terribly wrong to bring the newsboys all the way to their street, and in the dark. Mom and Aunt Bessie were crying. Dad and Uncle were clearly worried. And Ruthie's heart ached for her country, but she did not understand it at all.

Long into the night Dad and Uncle Charlie listened to the radio and talked together. Ruthie went to sleep listening to the rise and fall of their voices.

The next day at school there was a buzz of excitement.

"Did you hear . . . ?"

"Yeah . . . I know."

"My dad says . . ."

"Are you scared?"

"Will Milwaukee be bombed?"

"Hitler is crazy, and so are the Japanese."

All kinds of conversations buzzed all over the playgrounds and in the classrooms. The teachers did their best to keep the children's minds on their studies, but there was no denying the problem. It was not going to go away!

After several days things began to settle down. Oh, there was still a whole lot of trouble brewing, but somehow the teachers and the children could more easily focus their attention on their studies. The world had not yet come to an end, although trouble loomed on the horizon.

The students were aware of that. It was hard for them to keep their attention on the upcoming holiday season.

Winter had set in. Snow made everything white and beautiful. Walking to school was fun. The heavy snowfalls made every tree look as if it had been decorated.

Of course, Old Clyde, the janitor, shoveled the school's sidewalks, and Ruthie and Mary Ann could not help being amused by him. When it got severely cold, he wore his old black hat with the earflaps down. His mustache often froze, and he made an odd spectacle. But the girls were polite enough to wait until they were out of earshot before they giggled and made faces imitating how funny he looked.

"Do you think if he laughed his mustache would crack?" Mary Ann asked with a giggle, and Ruthie joined her.

Almost every day Dad and Uncle Charlie talked about the war. Ruthie often overheard them as she passed through the downstairs or as Uncle visited with Dad upstairs.

"I understand that Japan's goal in attacking Pearl Harbor was to weaken the U.S. fleet enough so that Japan could then attack and capture the Philippines and Indochina," Dad said. Ruthie, who was playing jacks on the floor, stole a quick look at her dad. His eyes were dark with worry.

"And more than that, Justus, more than that," Uncle replied. "Japan needs raw materials from those countries so that it can further extend its empire to include

Australia, New Zealand, and India. This is a war on a global scale."

Ruthie could not take it all in. This was too much to understand. At school the teacher had helped them look at a globe. The students put their fingers on the countries that were fighting. The little bit that was Japan seemed very far from Hawaii. How had they been able to fly so far with planes loaded with bombs? Robby had a theory about that, but even that was confusing.

Then Ruthie found Sicily and Italy. It seemed strange that when he was younger than Steve, Dad had taken a ship all the way from Sicily to New York. Italy was in the war too, and Dad worried about his family. It was all too scary to think about.

For just a moment Esther stood with her finger on Germany, then turned quickly away. Mrs. Armstrong was calling the class to order. Some of the other boys stretched out their arms and zoomed to their seats. "Bombs away!" Robby said, and everyone laughed.

Mrs. Armstrong stood at her desk not saying a word. When everyone was quiet, she said a few calming words about the fighting. Some of the students had relatives in the military or knew of others who did. And there was a rising spirit of patriotism among the people of the United States, the children as well as adults. After all, the United States had been attacked. An enemy had flown thousands of miles to drop bombs on a U.S. possession, and now the U.S. had joined the war. That fact alone seemed to draw everyone together.

FIFTEEN

Gimbel's Animal Show

Hundreds of parents and friends attended the school Christmas program. The large auditorium was filled, as almost everyone who had been invited turned out to support their children. Ruthie and her friends thought they'd never seen the auditorium look so pretty, decorated as it was for Christmas.

People tried to make things normal in their lives, even though that seemed impossible. Nothing was normal any longer. However, the adults knew that life would and must go on even though their country was at war. In fact, now that the U.S. had entered the war, people hoped that the U.S. soldiers could help the war end quickly.

"Your dress is beautiful," Esther told Ruthie as the students quietly took their seats. "I love those colors." One finger reached up and almost touched her friend's collar.

"Thank you," Ruthie said. "My mother crocheted the lace. You can touch it if you want."

Esther's finger traced the scalloped edge. "My grandmother used to crochet," she said. "Till her hands got too old."

"That's too bad."

"I know. But she's *really* old."

When it came time for her choral group to sing, Ruthie breathed deeply, then confidently strode to stand before the seated choir. She waited a moment before raising her hand—the cue for the group to stand. Their eyes were riveted upon her as they waited for the signal from her baton. Then as she directed, they sweetly sang,

"'The snow's on the mountain, the snow's in the glen,
And Christmas has come to our glad hearts again . . .'"

When the music ended, the applause was loud and strong. Ruthie turned and bowed with her classmates. Then they returned to their places.

Chicago Symphony, Ruthie thought to herself.

"Our class took the show," Doris whispered to Ruthie when they were seated. They grinned at each other and for a moment clasped hands.

❦

Everyone welcomed Christmas vacation. Almost two weeks out of school!

"See you at the Tree-Trunk Show!" Robby shouted as he ran out into the snow-frosted schoolyard. "Don't be late."

Ruthie and Mary Ann decided to go to the Gimbel's show on the first day of the big event, even if it was going to be very crowded.

Just before they left, Mom handed Ruthie a small change purse.

"Now, put this in your pocket, and take care not to

lose it. It is seven dollars to buy yourself those figure skates you've been wanting. It's your Christmas present from Gen and Steve and Dad and me."

"Oh, Mama!" Ruthie exclaimed. "How wonderful. Thank you. Thank you!"

"Just be sure to get a size larger than your shoes so your feet will have room to grow. Now go and have fun." Mom gave her a hug and kissed the top of her head.

Ruthie and Mary Ann jumped on the streetcar. They talked all the way, so it seemed that in no time at all the streetcar turned onto Wisconsin Avenue. They would soon be there.

Gimbel's entire store was filled with people. The auditorium on the third floor became packed as well. But the girls had left home early so that they could get there early, so they got great seats and could see every act.

And right behind them sat Esther and her younger brother.

Esther leaned forward and lightly touched her school friend. "Ruthie," she said in her soft way, "this is my brother, Thad. Thad, this is Ruthie."

"Nice to meet you," said young Thad. Then recognition lit up his face, and his eyes sparkled. "Oh, you're Ruthie. My sister's special friend." He looked back at his sister for confirmation. Esther nodded. Her eyes looked more sad and sober than they ever had before.

Somehow the look in Esther's eyes made Ruthie uneasy. She'd sensed from the first that this awful war frightened Esther more than it did her other classmates. Ruthie did not understand why. Mom had told her that all one could do was pray that the good Lord would watch over the situation. And pray for a soon end to the war.

Ruthie smiled at both of them. "It's nice to meet you, too, Thad."

Before the show began, the president of Gimbel's announced the winner of the Name the Elephants contest. In a loud, dramatic voice he announced, "Their names will be—Gimbie and Ellie!"

Everyone clapped. Some of the boys even shouted and whistled. The child who had won the contest was from the city's south side, so Ruthie and Mary Ann didn't know him at all.

"Aw shucks, Mary Ann. Robby's names sounded just as clever," Ruthie sighed.

"*Better*, I'd say," agreed Mary Ann; then they settled down to watch the show.

Oh, it was fun. Right in the auditorium were the two elephants, and they carefully walked on wooden planks. There were dogs that did tricks and a clown who performed a lot of funny magic acts. Then there was a small pony show with a pony that was smart as any dog, and a man who walked on stilts. The background music to all these acts was peppy and lively.

But the animal act that surprised Ruthie and Mary Ann the most was the cat show. In between various parts of the program, cats ran here and there. Sometimes they were holding up announcement banners or running up to the rooftops of the props and pretending to dim the lights. One cat even walked a tightrope. That was a sight to see!

After the show Ruthie went to the athletic department and bought her skates.

"Look at them, Mary Ann. The white leather, the shiny blades! Ooooo, I love them," Ruthie said, hugging the box to her chest.

Then she and Mary Ann went to the toy department and joined the crowd of kids who were watching the train exhibit. The whole train table had been decorated to look like a miniature village. There were small houses and trees and bridges. Model trains chugged around the tracks, stopping at a small station, then whistling and moving on. With several trains speeding along at the same time, the children watched excitedly, wondering if there would be a collision on the various tracks.

Robby and Jerry were at the train table too.

"How about those names, Robby?" Ruthie asked him. "They weren't nearly as clever as yours."

Robby shrugged. "Well, they had to get the name of the store in there somewhere," he replied, "but yeah, I agree. Mine were better." He threw back his head and laughed.

SIXTEEN

Ruthie Does It

Early on, as Mom planned the Thirteenth Sabbath program, she decided that some of the younger children should have the opportunity to take part too. So she planned to put together a girls' trio. Mary and Josie were about the same age as Ruthie, and Mom had heard them sing. She felt certain the three girls would be able to harmonize well.

Josie had thick brown braids, sparkling brown eyes, and perfect pitch. When she started practicing with the trio, she amazed them all with her talent for harmony. Mary—the lucky girl—had dark naturally wavy hair and a contagious smile on her sweet, round face. "She's cute as a bug's ear," Ruthie had heard her mother say to Aunt Bessie.

Whenever she heard a grown-up use that expression, Ruthie always wondered how cute a bug's ear could actually be. Who could see one, anyway?

One Friday night after the youth meeting Mom got the three girls together and gave them a songbook that was written for three-part harmony. She'd gone to the Sunday school supply store all the way downtown and found the special trio book.

"Let's try 'Away in a Manager,'" Mom told them, "as it is one carol that you already know." She sat down at the piano. "Now, Mary, you take the lead. Josie, follow the middle notes as second soprano, and Ruthie, you follow the bottom, the alto notes." Mom played each of their notes so they could hear them—the soprano note, the second soprano note, and the alto. Then she gave them a chord to start, and played while they sang.

It was an immediate success. The girls really enjoyed singing, and Mom was right. None of them had any trouble learning their parts. Their voices were well balanced. Since all three of them had a good ear for music, Mom said that they made good music together.

After this first practice they practiced every chance they got. They'd decided to sing "Fairest Lord Jesus" for the Thirteenth Sabbath program, but they enjoyed singing other songs in three-part harmony too.

The month passed in a flurry of happy events. First, school let out for Christmas vacation. All the students looked forward to Christmas—all but Esther. She'd told Ruthie that her family didn't celebrate Christmas. Instead, they celebrated a Jewish holiday called Hanukkah. It helped them remember the time that God caused one day's supply of oil for the Temple lamps to burn for eight days, until a new supply of oil was found.

Either way, the children were happy for time to be out of school and to play in the snow. Ruthie had something else to do, too. She kept going over the whole year's worth of memory verses, making sure that she still knew them all. Mom and Aunt Bessie encouraged her, urging her to say them aloud for them.

Then right before Christmas Gen and Steve arrived home from college. Ruthie jumped up and down with excitement when she saw them. Steve grabbed her and swung her around, and she squealed with joy. It was wonderful to have them back. In the evenings Steve joined Dad listening to the radio. And he and Gen spoke of college guys who were being drafted. That was a new word for Ruthie—drafted. Gen explained that it meant that the U.S. government had asked them to join the Army and they couldn't say no.

Christmas Day was a happy time. Ruthie loved the tree decorated with the small colored lights. And there was a small surprise or two, even though she'd already gotten her main present, her new skates.

Then it was the end of December and Thirteenth Sabbath.

It was time for the youth department to present a program for the entire church congregation. The children had practiced and practiced. Mom had spent hours making sure that everyone knew their part well and that the program would run smoothly.

The church filled right on time that Sabbath morning. When everyone was seated, Mom stood up. Then in her polite, well-poised manner she said, "Welcome to our special Thirteenth Sabbath program. The young people and I are happy you are here."

Then she gave the names of those who would be participating in the program and what they would do. "The program will continue without further introductions," she announced, and took her seat.

Mama looks so composed, Ruthie thought. *No wonder Dad says she is gracious.*

Josie reached over and squeezed Ruthie's hand, but didn't whisper a word. Mom never allowed that. Josie just looked wide-eyed, and Ruthie knew she meant "Take courage!"

Gen was one of the first to stand. She played a piano solo, "The Holy City."

"Usually people think of 'The Holy City' as a vocal solo," she'd said to Mom, "but why not let me play it on the piano?" And Mom agreed.

Joey, who was the same age as Ruthie, sang "Savior, Like a Shepherd Lead Us." She listened closely as he sang. "He's a natural," she said to herself. As he lifted his eyes near the close of the song, Ruthie was impressed. "He's sincere, too. He's not trying to be dramatic."

Tony played a trumpet solo, "O Come, All Ye Faithful." The notes rang loud and clear in the small church.

Mom had asked Rosie if she would sing "There's a Wideness." She had sung it for church once before, but Mom knew the members would love to hear her again. Rosie had a beautiful low voice, and that song suited her exactly.

"My own sister Hettie sang this song several times in our church in New London when she was young. Church members requested her to sing it," Mom had told Rosie.

"Hettie had a lovely low voice, just as you have."

Ruthie had memorized the words just because she loved them. No one had asked her to; she had just done it.

Ruthie also knew that when her aunt Hettie grew up she and her minister husband had accepted a call to be missionaries in Turkey. Sadly, Hettie died from complications of childbirth before they could leave the country. But several months later Uncle Claude had decided to go alone. He still felt that God was calling him to far-off Turkey. Ruthie never had met him, but deep inside she loved and admired him.

So as Rosie sang, Ruthie inwardly sang with her. "'There's a wideness in God's mercy, like the wideness of the sea . . .'" Oh, how she sensed the beauty of the message of the words.

Vince and Paul sang a duet, "To Do Thy Will," and then Steve told the historical background of the writing of the song "Silent Night."

After Ruthie, Josie, and Mary sang "Fairest Lord Jesus," it was Ruthie's turn. The time had finally come for her to recite all 48 memory verses for the entire year, texts and all.

So she stood up, took a deep breath, and began.

After church the grown-ups shook Ruthie's hand and told her they were proud of her. The kids gathered round and congratulated her.

"That took lots of time, didn't it?" said Tony. "When I was a kid, I was always happy just to have my weekly verse memorized." He grinned and tapped Ruthie on her head.

Josie's little brother, Sonny, pulled on Ruthie's hand. "I thought you might make a mistake when I made a funny face at you, but you didn't!" he said with a grin. He was a sunny little boy and full of pranks and mischief.

Josie caught her breath, and her eyes grew big with surprise. "You naughty boy!" she said, and nudged him with her elbow.

"Never mind," said Ruthie, returning the boy's grin. "I never even saw you."

Sister Katerina gave Ruthie a bear hug. "You reminded me of those Waldensian people of long ago who memorized chapter after chapter in the Bible. They weren't allowed to have Bibles, so that's how they spread the gospel to those who had no way of knowing what the Bible says." She gave Ruthie a little hug. "God bless you."

This was a new idea to Ruthie. She'd not had any thought of that before. Suddenly she realized that learning what the Bible said was meaningful and important for lots of different reasons.

Of course, almost everyone thanked Mom for her well-planned program and complimented her on how well the children had done. "The children worked very hard," she said. "I give them credit for that, and thank our Creator for His blessing."

"Whatever would our church do without you?" Vince told her, and the other young people nodded in agreement.

Mom had once more risen to the occasion. The loving leadership she gave in both the Chicago and the

Milwaukee churches touched the lives of many young people. Countless souls may well be in the kingdom of heaven because of her influence.

When Ruthie and her family got home from church, Mom handed her a small box.

"Hurry and open it," said Gen, excited by the surprise.

Carefully removing the lid, Ruthie discovered a small, gold lapel pin with the words "Honor Roll" embossed on it. She was delighted.

"This pin will always remind you of the wonderful project you undertook," Dad told her. "Not everyone can recite 48 memory verses, and I'm proud of you."

Suddenly Ruthie felt warm and happy. It had been a big job, and she didn't always enjoy practicing the verses. But to have Mom and Dad proud of her, and to have this lapel pin to remind her of her achievement, was something she never forgot.

"We're all proud of you," she heard Dad saying. "And above all, Jesus is pleased that you witnessed for Him in such a mighty way."

And now, many years later, Ruthie still has the pin.

SEVENTEEN

Surprise!

 January 1 brought a whole new year, but a year shadowed by the war in Europe. Ruthie's world changed when World War II began. People's conversations were sobering and serious. Her parents told her that things would be different, yet in her young mind she didn't completely understand it all.

It was said that the production of cars would be stopped so that the making of tanks and trucks could be given priority. All metal had to be used for the war effort. When Ruthie heard that, her hopes for a bicycle were dashed. She figured that if the U.S. could not make cars, certainly they wouldn't be making bicycles, either.

Although no battle was fought on home soil during World War II, many people had loved ones who were valiantly defending their country far away. More and more houses had small flags hanging in their windows, showing that someone from that household was in the war. Blue stars meant that someone was in the military, and many windows had more than one blue star. Gold stars told the sad story that a life had been given for freedom.

Buddy's uncle was drafted into the Army. Mary Ann's cousin joined the Navy. Fellows Ruthie knew personally were serving their country—Martin, Paul, Nick, Tony, and Philly. Only boys who were in college, especially those studying to be ministers, were deferred from serving. "Deferred" meant that they would not be drafted. Steve was going to be a minister, so he was deferred.

The hardships of a country engaged in a life-and-death struggle touched the lives of everyone. Gasoline, flour, sugar, and even the buying of shoes were rationed. Everyone was given a certain number of ration coupons that had to last a month.

Then there were the nights of practice blackouts, when every light in the house was turned off and all the shades were pulled down. Even though there were no enemy planes around, everyone had to practice in case there was an attack. No crack of light dared show, for fear that enemy planes would be able to see and bomb them. Even though they were only practicing, Ruthie knew that should a real blackout ever become necessary, the routine would be just the same.

Convoys of Army trucks rolled down Hopkins Street on their way to the armory. Newly inducted soldiers practiced marching along the side of the streetcar tracks. All traffic stopped for them.

Dad wondered what might be happening to his family in Sicily. But there was no way of finding out for sure, since mail was carefully censored. No war plans were ever allowed to be discussed by international mail.

Signs appeared in store windows: "Loose lips sink ships." This meant that if you let information slip out, it could cause bad things to happen. But Ruthie's favorite saying was with a serious picture: "Uncle Sam needs you!" In the picture the index finger of the white-bearded Uncle Sam pointed outward toward anyone reading the sign.

War songs became popular, and slogans abounded. Then people started seeing "Rosie the Riveter" posters put up around Milwaukee. These showed "Rosie" working with tools. So many men were in the military that women had to take over some of the jobs that men usually did.

It was a strange, new world, but patriotism was widespread. Everywhere, everyone supported the president and the cause. No one complained about any inconvenience, not even when tinfoil could no longer be used to cover candy, and tooth powder replaced toothpaste and was packed in cardboard cartons rather than metal tubes. All this seemed trivial and unimportant compared to the hardships of the men overseas.

Every week or so students who had loved ones in the military or relatives living in war-torn countries were given time in school to give reports to their classmates.

The grandparents of Ruthie's classmate Kira lived in Russia. One day Kira brought to school a doll that her grandmother had made and sent to her before the war began. The doll wore a Russian dress embroidered with bright colors, and was very pretty.

All the schoolchildren liked learning the songs from the Army, Navy, Air Force, and the Marines. Ruthie's favorite was the Navy song "Anchors Aweigh."

On Saturday nights the streets of downtown Milwaukee were crowded with servicemen in uniform.

They were going to the USO stations, where they could get a good meal and even some entertainment. Sailors from the Great Lakes Training Center seemed to be everywhere too. Soldiers, marines, and Air Force men walked the downtown streets on Saturday nights. Ruthie and her friends could identify each uniform and recognize the soldier's rank by their stripes or stars.

Young people grew up in a hurry. Both on farms and in the city, boys did the work of men. No one was excluded from doing the work that had to be done—not grown-ups, not children.

When Martin's family got word that he was never coming home again, the whole church mourned. Ruthie wondered how death could happen to fun-loving, friendly Martin with the sparkling eyes and wavy hair. Roy, the son of a church family in Chicago, was the next casualty that Ruthie heard about. Her young heart ached to hear such devastating news.

Each morning at school when the class would rise and repeat the Pledge of Allegiance together, Ruthie said it with a new understanding of what patriotism meant.

After the school year ended, both Gen and Steve had summer jobs in Wisconsin. Ruthie was so happy that they were home again. Then several weeks later something exciting happened right about suppertime.

One evening Mom casually asked, "Ruthie, would you please go down to the basement and get a jar of peaches?"

Ruthie put down the book she was reading and skipped down the back hall steps. She didn't notice that the whole family was quietly following behind her.

When Ruthie opened the basement door, she saw a bicycle—a full-size bicycle! It was even bigger than Buddy's. She caught her breath and wondered if she were seeing things. Then turning around, she saw her family standing behind her. Their faces were wreathed with smiles. "Whose bike is this?" she asked.

"Yours!" they cried. "Surprise!"

Ruthie was stunned. Then Gen and Steve explained that they had bought it from a friend just for her.

"Oh, thank you, thank you!" Ruthie gasped, trying to hug them all at once. Steve helped her carry the bike up the steps and out the back door.

When Mary Ann, Maxie, Gloria, Dutchie, and Buddy saw Ruthie riding on her bike, they came running and shouting, "Where did you get that bike, Ruthie? It's a beauty. Is it yours? May we have a ride?"

Of course, the first to get a turn was generous-hearted Buddy, who had waited long and patiently for Ruthie to fulfill her promise that if she ever got a bike, he would be the first friend to ride it.

That night, happily exhausted by excitement, fresh air, and exercise, Ruthie fell asleep kneeling by her bed. Mom found her there later and lifted her up and tucked her in. "Thanks, Mama," Ruthie whispered. She smiled. "Jesus answered my prayer for a bike. I knew He would."

The Rest of Ruthie's Story

Ruth had the surprise bicycle for years. In fact, one summer when Steve needed transportation while he was helping a minister in an evangelistic tent meeting, he rode that bike. It stayed in the family for more than 40 years.

Ruthie had a wonderful childhood. She and her friends could play outside all day long without fear of being harmed. Their parents did make them come inside, however, when it grew dark and the streetlights came on. While in grade school, Ruthie and Mary Ann heard the great Adventist preacher H.M.S. Richards speak in an auditorium in downtown Milwaukee.

In seventh grade Ruthie joined the students at the new 10-grade SDA church school that opened not far from her home. Just after Ruthie completed tenth grade, the family moved to Fresno, California, where her father became the pastor of a Fresno church. The eleventh grade found her at Fresno Union Academy, where she graduated two years later.

Ruthie's love of music provided her a lifetime of pleasure. While she was in the academy, she sang in a girls' trio that won first place in the annual student talent show. Both in academy and college she thoroughly enjoyed playing bass drum and cymbals in the school band. And she and Gen sang in EMC's a cappella choir.

After academy graduation Ruth worked for one year, then went to Emmanuel Missionary College, where she took the two-year secretarial course. EMC wasn't too far from Wisconsin, Ruthie's home state, where her sister, Gen, and her family lived.

It was at EMC that Ruth met Gene Merkel. They courted, and fell in love. When Gen learned that her "baby" sister was getting married, she invited Ruth and Gene to have their wedding in the church that she and her husband attended. Ruth liked that idea—getting married in the state she'd lived in until she was 16. Wisconsin still felt like home.

Their first two years of marriage Ruth and Gene lived in Japan, where Gene was a hospital corpsman in the U.S. Naval Hospital in Yokosuka. Then they moved back to Michigan. Gene again went to EMC, graduating two years later. During this time Ruth worked as secretary to the man who'd married them—Floyd Rittenhouse, who was now the college president.

Ruth and Gene had two daughters, Elaine and Marcia, who brought much happiness and excitement into their home. The family traveled across the country from coast to coast, as Gene attended professional meetings. They visited Yosemite National Park, Niagara Falls, Paul Revere's home in Boston, the Mojave Desert, and other points of historic interest. They also traveled to England

and saw where Grandfather Henry Parfitt had been born.

When her daughters grew up, Ruth went back to something she loved—working as a secretary. She served as secretary to two college presidents, W. Richard Lesher and Niels-Erik Andreasen. It was while working for Richard Lesher that Ruth finished her bachelor's degree in office management. Her boss presented her diploma, and Ruth's 5-month-old granddaughter, Erin, was in the audience for the occasion!

Fifty years have passed since Ruth and Gene married. They enjoy travel and taking cruises with friends they've known since college. Their three grandchildren also add fun and joy to their lives. And Ruth still enjoys music. Though she's a senior citizen now, Ruth plays the bass drum in her town's band—the Berrien Village Band. 🌼

More About Ruthie's World

Life during World War II

Just as Ruthie and her family had to get used to brushing their teeth with tooth powder that came in a cardboard box, Americans everywhere both gave up conveniences and collected things for the war effort. Here is a list of the kinds of things people donated and how they were used to help win the war.

- One old push lawn mower—six three-inch shells for guns
- One worn-out tire—rubber for 12 gas masks
- One old shovel—six hand grenades

Almost everything had a use, including used tin cans, toothpaste tubes, and pots and pans. The Boy Scouts collected so much waste paper in 1942 (150,000 tons) that the U.S. paper mills couldn't handle it. But by 1945 scrap material of all kinds was supplying much of the steel, half the tin, and half the paper that was needed to win the war.

Because of the war the government even had rules about how much material could be in women's dresses! Here were some of the rules for manufactured clothes.

- Hems could be no more than two inches deep.
- There could be only one pocket per blouse.

- No attached hoods or shawls on dresses.
- No cuffs on coats.
- Even the use of metal zippers and fasteners was restricted.

This Fabulous Decade, 1940–1950

- Why Esther was worried

Esther and her family had good reason to be worried about their family members who lived in Europe. While Hitler was in power, millions of Jews were arrested and placed in prisons called concentration camps. Most of them were executed or died of illness or starvation before the war ended.

- Hanukkah

Esther told Ruthie that she didn't celebrate Christmas. Because people who follow the Jewish religion do not believe that Jesus is the Messiah, they don't observe the holiday that honors His birth. Instead, many Jews observe Hanukkah. It is an eight-day celebration that often comes near Christmas. This religious holiday reminds them that during a war fought to destroy them, a small amount of oil burned for eight days in the Temple—until more oil finally arrived. This happened in a time period between the Old and New Testaments.

The word *Hanukkah* means "dedication," and reminds Jews to rededicate themselves to God. The only scripture that mentions Hanukkah is in the New Testament. Jesus went to the Temple during the Festival of Dedication,

143

which is another name for Hanukkah. The scripture is John 10:22.

After the War

Things changed after World War II ended. Of course, the soldiers came home. But there were other changes. Though television had been perfected by the early 1940s, it wasn't produced for home use until the war was over. It took several years before a lot of people bought TVs, but by the end of the 1940s they were getting popular. Howdy Doody was one of the first TV shows for children.

- Penicillin

The discovery and use of penicillin has made the difference between life and death for millions of people. Before penicillin, a scratch could turn into a killing infection. And strep throat and pneumonia were often fatal.

At first penicillin was used by the military to treat wounded soldiers. When the war was over, doctors had a new antibiotic—a miracle drug—with which to fight infection for everyone.

Homemade Beauty

Now girls and their moms could get permanents at home. This cost less than going to a beauty shop and was more convenient.

- Nylon

Wow! For the first time dresses and shirts could be washed and hung up to dry quickly. And they didn't wrinkle much, either.